CONQUERING
FEAR

A Cancer Survivor's Wisdom

DAVID BANTZ

ISBN: 978-1-4834-4559-5 (sc)
ISBN: 978-1-4834-4558-8 (e)

Library of Congress Control Number: 2016901129

Lulu Publishing Services rev. date: 02/09/2016

To Olivia, Lori, Jenny, and David

CONTENTS

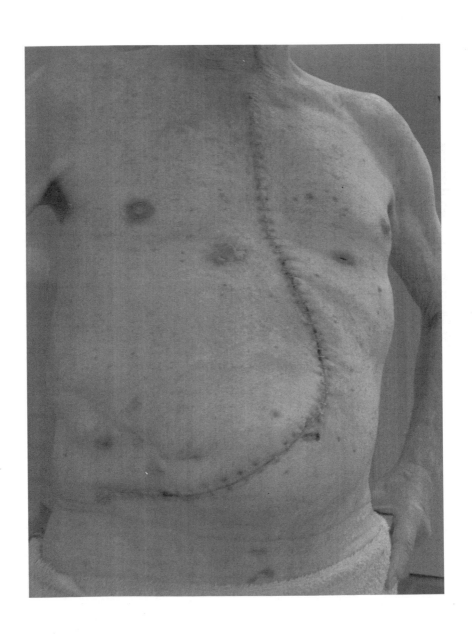

MEDICAL HISTORY

1986	Cancer	Adrenal cortical carcinoma (ACC) surgery. Dr. Brent Eastman (tumor - volleyball size)
1986	Surgery	Appendectomy (false alarm for recurrence of ACC).
1996	Cancer	Large squamous cell on face. Dr. Hugh Greenway (cell removal), Dr. Art Perry (reconstruction)
1998	Cancer	Adrenal cortical carcinoma (ACC) surgery. Dr. Peter Edelstein, colon resection, removed omentum (tumor - approximately the size of 2 tennis balls)
1998	Surgery	Repair abdominal hernias related to 1996 surgery. Dr. Dana Launer
1998	Cancer	Adrenal cortical carcinoma (ACC) surgery, removed kidney. Dr. Lee, M. D. Anderson (tumor - approximately the size of a golf ball)
2000	Surgery	Shoulder impingement surgery. Dr. Steve Shoemaker
2005	Surgery	Prostate surgery. Dr. Robert Hathorn
2006	Cancer	Basal cell on temple, neck, and below rib.
2007	Stroke	Lacuner infarct. Dr. Michael Lobatz
2008	Chondritis	Chondritis near thyroid. Dr. Marc Kramer
2009	Gout	Gout and chondritis near thyroid. Dr. Marc Kramer

on going	Sleep apnea	Severe (74%) obstructive sleep apnea, use of CPAP machine.
2010	Cancer	Cancer - adrenal cortical carcinoma. Surgery to remove 1/2 liver, gallbladder, 1/2 diaphragm, vena cava. Drs. Andrew Lowy, Alan Hemming, Michael Madani, and Fred Millard
2011	Cancer	Photodynamic therapy for spot on chest. Scripps
2011	Surgery	Surgery to remove/replace abdominal mesh, restructure abs & oblique muscles.
2012	Hematoma	Subdural hematoma. Dr. Robert Fox, St Mary's, Grand Junction, Colorado
2012	Surgery	Burr holes in skull. Dr. Justin Brown. Neurosurgeon, UCSD's Thornton Hospital
2013	Derm	Pseudomonas putida skin rash. Dr. Philip Cohen, UCSD
2014	Cancer, basal	Large basal cells on back, right temple under hairline, and upper arm. Dr. Brian Jiang

Family History

- Father died at age 57, stroke.
- Mother died at age 44, cancer.
- Sister (now age 83) had a major stroke at age 70.
- Brother died at age 55, accident.

THE GLASS OF WATER OVERFLOWING

This book is going to save lives—maybe yours. At the very least, it will enhance your life in ways you can't even begin to imagine. I know because I have the honor to have come under David Bantz's spell over the last two years, and working with him on *Conquering Fear - A Cancer Survivor's Wisdom* has caused a quantum shift in the way I look at myself and those around me that I love and how I relate to the world in general. If he's had that effect on me, I promise his book will do the same for you.

David and I were high school classmates back in 1960. I interviewed him in 2013 for *Turning Pages,* a film about some of our classmates and what had happened to them in the half century since graduation. In that film, he revealed his extraordinary odyssey of survival, revival, and rejuvenation. He revealed that he wanted to write a book to help others facing some of the same challenges he has—a thirty-year journey that most people would think could only be summarized as hell on earth—a nightmare of deadly illnesses, including four life-threatening cancer challenges, a stroke, and a subdural hematoma between the ages of forty-two and sixty-five. I told him I wanted to be his guide through the process of communicating what he'd learned.

In my writing career, I've interviewed more than 4,000 people, but I quickly discovered that in all my interviews with world-famous people, never had I met a person that more fascinated me than David Bantz. David is an engaging and avuncular personality. He's not a writer, per se. And he's certainly not a professional psychologist. Neither he nor I saw my role as a ghost writer. This would not be an as-told-to tome. We agreed that I would be his Sherpa guide, that we would climb this Mount Everest of a book together. I would be a mentor, a cheerleader, a compass.

David does not pontificate about therapies learned in a classroom. The strength of his position is that of someone who is living proof that late-stage cancer is not an end but another facet of life's journey. David told me he was determined to die *with* his cancer, not *from* it. That is only part of his message to you as he also lays out his way of achieving his goal.

In our weekly phone sessions, which were intended to be my critique of his writing, I found that all lines between mentor and student disappeared. David was changing my life for the better, while I was working to help him zero in on those philosophies of his life that were making my personal world more fulfilling—and could have a life-changing effect on uncounted numbers of others.

I didn't have cancer, but I am a Vietnam veteran who lived through sixty years of my mother's terror as a breast cancer "survivor" in name only. She was constantly terrified of the disease's return and of life. David is not terrified of his life. He's taught me not to be, and this book will show you how to experience joy every day, regardless of your personal demons. I'm a different person as a result of my odyssey with David, and you will be too when you read this book. David and I both see *Conquering Fear* now as far more universal than when we started. No one who reads this will be untouched.

Don Wilcock
Freelance Writer
Senior Editor - *The Audiophile Voice* Magazine
Contributing Writer - *Nippertown*
Contributing Writer - *The American Blues Scene*
Contributing Editor - *The Blues Music Magazine* (formerly *Blues Revue Magazine*)
Winner of The Blues Foundation's Keeping The Blues Alive in Print Journalism Award

PREFACE

I am a very lucky guy! I've had cancer for twenty-eight years. The next few paragraphs will give you a thumbnail sketch of the chart above, but the book explains how I managed to persevere and overpower fear through each of these challenges.

The chart is what my wife and I carry in our wallets in case I need medical treatment. It's a quick summary of the past twenty-eight years of my life from a purely medical point of view. Eventful. But my life has not been about all that. My life has been about my kids and family, my profession, sports, friends, and travel. You see, I am actually a very healthy guy now at age seventy, even through all those medical events. I play golf regularly, ski like a nut two or three times a year, travel extensively, and have a lot of fun with friends and family.

Oh, I do go to the doctor for checkups and the occasional treatment, but I fit those in around the other things. Some treatments take longer than others; yes, I have had four major cancers, a stroke, and a subdural hematoma. But, counterintuitively, rather than feeling loss, I feel I have gained a lot from those experiences. I survived multiple life-or-death situations by refusing to be overwhelmed. Fear is an easy associate but is in no way a friend.

During my engagements with cancer, I found I had learned ways of thinking, a group of thinking patterns I named My Chi, which enabled me to choose to embrace rather than fight my cancer. This overall way of thinking and using My Chi allowed me to own my cancer and resolve over and over to live with my cancer rather than die from it. As I was not in control of the length of my life, I chose to strive to live life with grace. I found that choice lets me live out my life with peace of mind.

This book is my offer to you, the reader, to benefit from how those kinds of experiences made me a stronger and happier person. The joy of life every day, no matter what it may bring, is the way I live now.

Okay, so my 1986 cancer and a false alarm later that year changed my life. Looking back, I think the change was for the better. Then, ten years later, I started experiencing intermittent and increasing pain in my back. Some of us sports guys do not pay a lot of attention to that, but it kept getting worse and was in the center of my back, not a usual place for a muscle pain. One day, it was so bad that I had to go to the ER. The docs did a scan and called Dr. Wayne Hooper, my wonderful primary doc, who met us there and told us that, indeed, it appeared to be cancer again. I guess I was expecting it to reappear, but after ten years, I thought maybe it wouldn't.

So started a flurry of appointments to plan the approach. Quickly, we found a surgeon who would operate. We scheduled that. On the operating table, my body again contorted. The doctors were able to remove a tumor along with part of my colon and intestines, and put me back up "among the vertical." They also removed the omentum, protective abdominal tissue, from my abdomen, thinking that might take away more lingering cancer cells than they could see. I healed quickly (one of the great benefits of being in shape) and got back to life as usual.

Since I had a new major cancer on my record, the screenings became more frequent, and two years later, more pain and additional scans showed that the cancer was back yet again, and this time on my right kidney and vena cava. Yikes, a bad one. The terrific surgeon who had done the 1996 surgery had left San Diego, and we were referred to M.D. Anderson, a well-known, large cancer center hospital in Houston, Texas. After gathering huge amounts of medical records, we flew to Houston and met with the doctor, who agreed to try a very complicated surgery.

Adrenal cortical carcinoma (ACC) is a slow growing and rare cancer. It occurs in about one in a million people, so there are only about three hundred cases in the United States and just a few others documented around the world. Even now, there are few studies and little documentation about ACC. In those still fairly early days of the Internet, my wife, Olivia, who before marriage was the detail person of our business partnership, pored over websites trying to find information and found one report that she passed on to one of the doctors, who agreed to expedite the surgery.

It was a long and arduous surgery resulting in a long, half-moon-like incision curling around my abdomen just below my rib cage. I actually lost my belly button in the process. The surgeon found he had to remove a kidney that was sharing blood supply with the tumor he removed. It was a tough recovery. It takes the body a while to transfer all functions to the other kidney, and I dealt with internal swelling, including pressure on a nerve that resulted in about ten days of double vision. Very disconcerting. We stayed in Houston all that time, and the doctors and ophthalmologists were great. Then home again, and we were back to work and normal life within three weeks. I just am not built, either physically or mentally, to sit around.

Regular scans followed for a few years, and it seemed that I again might really be in the clear. I had a shoulder surgery unrelated to cancer, and life moved on. We had a lot of fun, bought a second (now primary) home in the mountains, skied and golfed a lot, traveled to wonderful destinations, and worked very hard, very long but fulfilling hours.

In 2007, we were wrapping up a weekend at our mountain home when I got a funny tingling in my fingers and called to my wife. She calmly said, "You are having a stroke." Of course, I denied it, and she pulled from the inside door of a kitchen cabinet an article on the warning signs of stroke. Why did she have that right at hand? Amazing. I continued to deny it, though my speech was slurred, I had a sudden headache, I couldn't raise my arms to the same level, and the tingling progressed to numbness in my fingers. Since we were just about to drive back to town, Olivia continued the packing process, and we left in about fifteen minutes. (She knew that we had about three hours to get to a stroke-center hospital to be evaluated for possible use of the clot-buster drug.)

Olivia is usually the driver in our family, as she admits that she is a very bad passenger. I like to fiddle with the radio too much. So I usually do that and nap while she drives. She told me en route that we were going to the hospital, but I said no, I'd be fine. Nevertheless, she went to the hospital. The ER was empty, and the medical staff also clearly saw the signs of stroke and got me right in. Scans were done and evaluated quickly. Yes, I'd had a small stroke but significantly bigger than a transient ischemic attack (TIA). I stayed in the hospital for about forty-eight hours and was released, blessedly, with no deficits—that is, I got back to normal quickly with virtually no effects.

My sister had had a very debilitating stroke about seven years earlier, and my father had died from a stroke at age fifty-six, so I knew it ran in the family. I have high blood pressure, which I monitor and successfully medicate. The only trigger that we can figure out is that I had sneezed about five times (very big sneezes), which caused the infarct. Now when I sneeze more than twice, Olivia immediately gets upset and tells me to *stop*!

In the summer of 2008, I started getting very serious pain in the shoulder where I'd had a surgery. I went back to the shoulder doc, who sent me to a neck doc, who sent me to a neurologist, who sent me to a neurosurgeon, who sent me back to the shoulder doc. I'm sure you have had that sort of experience, too. No one could find anything wrong. It was a debilitating pain in the nerve over my right scapula and sometimes would take two days to diminish. I'd even have to leave work, stop a golf game, or suffer if we were traveling—and no one could find the cause. It was the worst pain I'd ever had, and it was so frustrating that we could not find the cause or even the triggers. It persisted with no answers through the rest of 2009.

Meanwhile, though my partners kindly wanted me to continue, I really wanted to enjoy life without the pressure of worrying about work. In December 2009, just after my sixty-fifth birthday, I retired.

At the same time, Dr. Hooper once again wanted me to go to a hematologist because of an anomaly in my blood work. The new doc was very kind. She took some more blood and said she would get back to us after her Christmas vacation. But after two months of waiting for her office to give us information, we moved on. We looked elsewhere for diagnosis and discovered I once again had a large, cancerous growth in my abdomen. This led to an incredible half-year-long search far and wide for a doctor willing to operate. I was viewed by doctor after doctor as inoperable with a year and a half to two years to live, even with chemotherapy.

I'm still here to write this book for you, so you know the story ends well. You don't need to read the last chapter of this book first, like my wife does when she reads a thriller because she can't stand the suspense. But I must say she handled well the suspense and latent fears we lived with during most of 2010 while trying to find that one doctor who would finally say, "Yes, I will do the operation."

Now that you have a general idea of the progression of my medical events, it's time to tell you what these experiences made me think, what I learned, and how I made my way through these trials to have a very normal life. Really.

And maybe, just maybe there are some thoughts I've had about these episodes that can give you a lift when you are facing a seemingly insurmountable challenge in your life.

Cheers,
David

CHAPTER 1

KITES RISE AGAINST THE WIND

Kites rise against the wind. No man has ever worked his passage anywhere in a dead calm.

— John Neal

My first thought was, *Oh no! How can this be happening? I am way too young for this at forty-two years old, and I have a wife and two small kids!*

Just a few hours earlier, a dreaded but miraculous series of events began rapidly unfolding that would take me to the depths of life and eventually to the heights. My wonderful doctor, W. Wayne Hooper, a top-drawer pulmonologist here in San Diego County, said he felt I might be dealing with something more than what we thought was walking pneumonia. I remember it well. He said, half joking, "Dave, if I didn't know you so well, I'd think these symptoms and blood tests indicate your body is fighting something other than pneumonia." He then froze for a moment and started feeling just below my diaphragm in my abdomen. His expression darkened as he found something hard and massive that, as I've said many times since, wasn't supposed to be there.

This was 1986—before a lot of the sophisticated tests and remarkably accurate scans we now have for cancer were available. Dr. Hooper quickly referred me to a surgical group that confirmed his suspicions through a sonogram like those used in viewing a fetus during pregnancy. What they found was shocking to all of us. I was dealing with a sizable (just a bit smaller than an irregularly shaped volleyball) cancerous growth that was

1

pushing up on my diaphragm and right lung. It had completely engulfed my right adrenal gland and attached itself to my liver, intestines, and right kidney as well as my vena cava, the garden-hose-sized vein that returns blood from the legs to the heart. All this obstruction was causing the pneumonia-like symptoms I hadn't been able to shake.

A whirlwind three days later, I lay on an operating table in a position that made me look like a Pillsbury dough can after opening. A group of surgeons cut an upward-spiral, thirty-plus-inch incision from the front of my pelvis around to my backbone and up between my shoulders. They then removed one of my ribs to create room to remove as much as possible of the mostly encapsulated tumor from my right abdomen.

People with my kind of cancer have an average survival rate of about two years after discovery. Life expectancy after five years is about 20 percent. They don't usually hang around for more than twenty-five years, as I have been so fortunate to do.

The roller coaster had begun. Cancer? Bad news. Surgery? Successful, and therefore, good news. But since the doctors realized it had been there long enough to attach to several vital organs, they warned us that there were likely cancer cells left behind that could develop in the future.

Now that's bad news. Certainly it was in the short term. I had no way to know the truth at that time, but as I look back twenty-eight years later, was it? In fact, I had been saved from certain death by being directed to and agreeing to have a massive surgery. How incredibly fortunate! And surgery had been done by some masterful surgeons. Again, how incredibly fortunate!

But then, limbo. I probably still had cancer. The surgical recovery was tough, but the thought of an enemy possibly still growing quietly in my body was terrifying. I asked myself how I could manage the fear.

My brain began processing these thoughts during the months I was recovering from the surgical ordeal. Facts I knew included a gentle statement from my oncologist to my wife and me that, thanks to the surgery, I probably had a year and a half, maybe a bit more, to "organize my affairs." Months later, in October 1986, as if to confirm the inevitable, the doctors scanned me and said it might be growing again. So we decided to operate—again.

And again, good fortune and blessings arrived at my bedside. It was only scar tissue. I could have been angry at the unnecessary surgery, but instead I found a way to be grateful. These people had already saved my life once. And I was learning fast how insidious and tricky cancer can be, both for the patient and the doctors. At least while they were in there, they removed my appendix to reduce some risk of recurrence in that area. This was the second major surgery I had to recover from within a year. Good grief. What was the rest of my life, however long, going to be like?

I look back and realize that so much of life is counterintuitive. At that time, I had no idea how powerful those events, all the conversations, and those days of thought were in forming the trajectory of the rest of my life experience. And I did not have any idea that this and other negative and traumatic events very early in life, such as losing loved ones, would oddly strengthen me. Later, they acted as a wonderful inoculation against the powerfully negative aspects of being a perilously at-risk, but now determined to be continuous, cancer survivor. As I mentioned, I write this having had my seventieth birthday.

What follows is not a biography or chronological tale of my continuing bouts with cancer (yes, the docs were right, and I had many more surgeries, which I will mention in context with my thoughts in this book). Instead, this is my effort to share with you, as a friend would, my journey of thought and emotional growth as challenges in my life, physical and otherwise, have occurred.

I am not a psychologist and so have not written about my coping mechanisms from a clinical point of view. I was just as terrified about the *C*-word as you are, but I was able to put that fear to work and not let it consume me. My goal is to offer you those skills that I learned in living with cancer.

Each challenge, it turns out, has given me the opportunity to grow and discover powerful ways of thinking and adapting. Change is inevitable. It is how we react to each change that determines the quality of the outcome. As former United Nations Secretary General Dag Hammarskjold said many years ago, "We are not permitted to choose the frame of our destiny. But what we put into it is ours." We really do have choices, even when it seems there are none. It is my hope that by sharing with you my experiences and discoveries, you, too, can begin to see your choices when it may seem initially that there are none.

Fear Is a Great Motivator

My main goal in this book is to sensitize you so you can be aware of and enable an amazing part of yourself that will empower your thoughts when change occurs, to achieve desirable results rather than the results we at first fear. I vividly remember the moments of fear I experienced each time my cancer reappeared in my body. But fear is a great motivator. It's counterintuitive, but we can channel that fear to create a positive outcome. I have encouraged myself to learn how to deal with the feeling of fear, and at times, instead of attempting to overpower it, I have befriended and incorporated it into my life.

Embracing Cancer

I have chosen to embrace my cancer and, with that, the accompanying fear. By embracing cancer, I mean I accept it willingly. While I can't rid myself of it, I have found I can manage it and empower myself to do things I might not have done without that motivation.

The problem we humans have is that fear normally drives us to react immediately and emotionally, sometimes with panic. In fact, when fear arises, those are the reactions of most species in the animal kingdom, but they are rarely the best choices upon review. Living with and befriending the fear can yield marvelously positive results.

People kindly say nice things about my successful efforts to survive, but I believe I am not any different from them or you. Really, it has been my good fortune to have discovered patterns of thinking through dealing with my ongoing cancer and some other exceptional challenges. I believe these patterns of thinking are at the root of success in anything. Over time, I have broadened the use of these thought patterns and found them to be powerful, whatever the endeavor.

Ever heard the cliché "Whatever doesn't kill you will make you stronger?" Do you believe it? I think the reason it is still used today is that with the right

4

thinking, you become stronger for having faced a challenge and dealt with it successfully. The key aspect is self-talking your way to a positive outcome.

My personal case in point? Well, as I said, I am seventy years old. I was forty-two the day Dr. Hooper found my massive tumor. Ah, but my most recent and fourth major cancer surgery was just three and a half years ago. I have taught my mind to retrieve and believe my five favorite mottoes:

> Keep on keepin' on. —Anonymous

> Do that thing you fear most and the death of fear is certain. —Mark Twain

> I will live with this cancer rather than die from it! —David Bantz

> Obstacles are those frightful things you see when you take your eyes off your goals.—Henry Ford

> The best way to predict the future is to create it. —Prof. Peter Drucker

I believe I have enough years and experiences that I can confirm these sayings/mottoes are powerful affirmations.

In short, if I am successful with this message, you will finish the last chapter with the ability to deal positively with seemingly major setbacks in your life—like discovering that you have cancer. You will begin to see recurring patterns of thought you can manage and therefore take action to improve the outcome of the challenges in your life.

Fear can cause panic and reactive, ill-considered responses. Or counterintuitively, you can see rising fear as an indicator of an opportunity for you to rise above and use mental "tools." With what follows, I will lay out experiences in my life to allow you to see how you might arm yourself with those same skills inside your head. If I am successful, you will begin to embrace life's challenges rather than fear them, as I did. You will use them as encounters to move forward to increase happiness and peace of mind in your life.

Welcome to my world for a few hours.

CHAPTER 2

YOUR CLOSEST FRIEND

All that we are is the result of what we have thought. The mind is everything. What we think, we become.

—Buddha

Watch your thoughts, they become words;
Watch your words, they become actions;
Watch your actions, they become habits;
Watch your habits, they become character;
Watch your character, for it becomes your destiny.

—Frank Outlaw
Late president of the Bi-Lo Stores, May 1977

Psychologists call the silent conversation we have with ourselves "self-talk." It is a potent force in our lives. Self-talk is with us every day, every hour, and every waking minute. It's a little bit like "you are what you eat." You are what you think, too. When we comment to ourselves about our actions, our mind takes what we're thinking (self-talking) literally. We are hardwired that way. Like our dreams, we cannot rid ourselves of them, so we need to be aware of them and make best use of our mental structure. It is a potent force in our lives.

Self-talk is a mental activity. It translates into feelings, which, if they become powerful, drive us to do things. Self-talk is a force that creates feelings that cause positive or negative action. Importantly, we have that choice. While I may not have a conscious choice about what I dream, I have found I really do have a choice when it comes to my self-talk. By turning my self-talk positive, I can encourage myself to do things from a base of courage and patience rather than fear and panic.

During my days, weeks, and months of knowing I was living with a large and growing cancer inside me, you can imagine how potent self-talk was. Whether you have had to deal with cancer or not, I'm sure you can imagine how quickly negative thoughts and fears would begin to creep into my mind. We with cancer have self-talk moments that demand we face up to the fear of death if we fail.

It was during these times I became aware of my self-talk and made the enormous discovery that I could develop the skill and art of managing my self-talk not only during these tough cancer years, but also beyond. Self-talk is such a part of us, it is as unconscious in our minds as breathing. But we can change and manage our breathing if we actively think about it. This is true for our self-talk, too.

Occasionally, I could just hear the dark voices of my doubt talking. I learned over time that I had to make an active choice to adjust when that happened. I had to redirect my negative self-talk to quickly replace those fearful thoughts. They were, as one sports psychologist said via an acronym, False Expectations Appearing Real (FEAR) in our minds. I actively chose to think of a positive outcome. So I began actively choosing to think of myself happily seeing my kids playing soccer the next year or graduating from high school, rather than fearing that those moments would never come. Eventually, I gave myself permission to say *What the heck, I'll think really positively and envision myself congratulating my daughter and son as they graduate from a university.* And years later, I did, with both of them.

Don't Think about Pink Elephants!

Aha! You thought of pink elephants. This is among the common and fun exclamations we can use as a way of showing that our brains cannot execute a negative command. This is different than thinking negative thoughts in our self-talk. I know it's confusing, but a negative command is slightly different than a negative thought or train of thought.

We can engage in a negative stream of thought and this evolves into feelings of fear, as when I didn't control my self-talk about cancer. Thinking or saying, "Oh my gosh, I am going to die," would be horribly self-defeating if left unchecked. But I'm changing the subject a bit here. When I tell you not to think of pink elephants, that is a negative instruction. The inability of the brain to execute a negative command or instruction is mechanical. It is related to but different than thinking negatively. It can be just as self-defeating if we don't reckon with it.

"Don't hit it in the water!" is a golfer's frequent self-admonition (negative command) just before hitting his driver off the tee or his nine iron over the water by the green. The last thing the brain hears is *water*. It thinks water. It fears water. The brain's owner tightens up his muscles in his hands and arms as he reacts to his self-talk and … hits it in the water. Almost all sports psychologists say the percentage chance the golfer will hit it in the water significantly increases with this negative self-talk instruction.

The remedy is to choose to focus on positive swing thoughts or instructions such as "I will keep my head still" or "aim for the grass on the fairway." These are positive instructions the mind can execute and they eliminate the negative "don't hit it in the water." This classic analysis of self-talk is backed up by substantial studies. Using positive self-talk in the form of positive swing thoughts is a good rule for the golfer and all of us in general. We need to monitor our self-talk and think positive instructions when attempting any physical effort.

Now let's broaden this discussion of self-talk to other situations where we are not dealing with commands to ourselves, just self-conversation. If we fall into the rut of noticing even the smallest of our slips and failures and saying negative things to ourselves about ourselves, guess what we hear and what our mind begins to believe? Example: You drop your fork on the restaurant floor with a loud clatter, and everyone seems to be looking at you as you sheepishly pick it up. As you do so, you cannot help but say to yourself, "You clumsy idiot!"

If you go from that small moment to saying things like that to yourself every time you make a mistake, you may find over time your thoughts become negative feelings about yourself. You don't respect yourself. If you are disrespecting yourself, how can you expect others to respect you? You may say, "I can't control my mind and its thoughts; it's self-talk." Well,

I say you're right that you can't control it, but you can manage it. This is similar to dealing with our investments. While we can't eliminate risks we take when investing, we can manage the amount of risk we take and therefore minimize the risk we take.

We can't truly control our breathing and change it forever, but we can actively manage it and change it for a while whenever we wish by actively engaging ourselves in the process. Similarly, we can learn to listen to our self-talk and "correct" it.

Is there a big reward if we actively manage our self-talk toward its positive version? From my experience, yes. There is the potential that we will feel better every day if we adjust what feeds our self-talk. But we have to train ourselves to recognize negative self-talk and turn it into positive self-talk before it is magnified into negative feelings. Even when we have the most minor self-talk, we can replace a self-insult with a forgiving or even positive rejoinder; maybe something like, "I may be an idiot, but I'm good at recovering quickly." You are not denying the negative moment, but now you have immediately used your self-talk management to refocus on a positive thought about yourself and created positive rather than negative feelings from the experience.

Catch the Fear

From the moment we arise in the morning, our self-talk begins. Do you find your talk to be mainly positive or do you hear yourself dreading things and saying negative things about your ability to deal with the events of the coming day? This is a prime opportunity for you to examine your self-talk.

Imagine if you become able to start your day with positive, forward-thinking self-commentary, maybe still with trepidation about some of your tougher challenges in the coming day, but you catch yourself and choose to be positive. But you still find yourself saying, "Oh no. This is the day I have to make that big presentation." Now catch the fear! Think about how to reduce the fear with a positive. Confront and adjust your self-talk. "So I will make time to study my notes two more times before the meeting. That way I will be more confident and do better."

Now, as you shower and get ready for the day, you are heartened and reassured by your self-talk. Any feelings of fear start to recede. You find you are refocused on the positive of making time to study your notes. Focusing on these steps calms you until you do the studying. You are no longer focused on fear of not being prepared for the meeting. You are focused on the positive of preparation. This self-talk is reinforced as you actually find the time you need. Resulting confidence inspires positive self-talk, which in turn spurs you to do your best.

I found that managing my self-talk to look for the good in life has universal applications, not just in managing my cancer. Presentations may not be a part of your life, but you may be a student or interviewing for a job. The same pattern of thought I laid out above for preparation for a meeting could be used to reassure yourself by studying your notes before taking an important exam or meeting a potential employer.

If you are a salesman and you have an appointment with an ornery client later in your day, focusing your self-talk on what you can do to offset any complaints will calm and reassure you.

As you will sometimes hear people say, words matter. I change the word in my self-talk from "problem" to "challenge" or "opportunity." Sounds corny but it works with self-talk. "I have a problem" is just not as easy to deal with as "I have a challenge." I then try to come up with answers to each challenge before a meeting. As I do this, I cannot help but feel better for exercising my self-talk in this positive direction rather than just dealing with feelings of fear and foreboding. Maybe you've heard the cliché, if you're going to bring me a problem, bring me solutions, too. If you train and manage it, your self-talk will do this for you every time.

No one can start catching your deleterious self-talk for you. Just like learning to ride a bike, this is a personal effort that starts with very small steps that can only be made by you. So when you put this book down, don't put yourself down. As you start to do something else, immediately listen to how you phrase your self-talk in the next experience of your day.

People say a valued trait in a friend is the ability to be a good listener. Be a good friend to yourself. Listen to yourself, and, like a good friend, evaluate what you hear and gently adjust your negative self-talk into positive statements. Don't deny it, change it. Sounds childish, and the first few times, it may feel just like the first time you rode a bike. I challenge you to try it, do it more than a few times and see how you begin to feel.

Self-talk takes on larger and longer-term forms, too. Closely related to this concept of self-talk is the critical ability to define who you are, rather than be defined by others. During one of his presentations, a master in the area of self-improvement, Jack Canfield, addressed a young lady in the front row of his audience. It went approximately like this:

"Miss, I like your brown shoes."

She responded, "Thank you, Dr. Canfield, but they are blue."

Jack responded immediately and firmly. "I think they are brown."

Flustered, she said just as firmly, "But they are blue, Jack."

This was the key moment for Canfield. He pointed out to the audience how committed the young woman was when it came to the color of her shoes. In general terms, he said to her (and the rest of the audience), the next time you find someone trying to incorrectly define who you are or saying something negative about you that you know to be untrue, you need to be just as firm. Do not be swayed by others' opinions of you. You know the color of your shoes without doubt. You should have as much confidence in your knowledge of yourself. Use self-talk to reaffirm it.

Big Brother

If we teach ourselves to do so, we can advance through life with greater confidence and achieve our goals sooner. This was a hard lesson for me. I had another layer to deal with that infected my self-talk. My brother was

11

a really great brother. When I was a kid in his backyard—that's the way the yard felt to me if he was there—he played with me a lot. He could have ignored me because he was six years my senior and successful in so many ways. But instead, we played, and he taught me many things.

Succinctly, he became my idol. Over the next twenty years, I let him define me in family situations and even in social situations. My self-talk was all about trying to be like him. This was different and separate from my true brotherly love for him, but I did not understand that back then. He was a great high school athlete. In his twenties and thirties, he became a remarkably successful Madison Avenue advertising executive. He was part of the team of executives responsible for putting the first issue of *People* magazine on the newsstands.

In the 1950s and '60s, as his younger brother watching him in self-talk terms, I chose to defer to him and try to be a copy of him. In other words, he was my idol and now my model, too. My self-talk was driving me to strive for a false goal. I was filled with negative self-talk because I could not duplicate him; I could never catch up to his performance any more than I could catch up to him in age. Still, I copied his mannerisms and objectives, feeling that if I could imitate him I, too, would be as successful. Little did I know that I was simply delaying discovery of myself. There was no such thing as my being able to achieve what I perceived as his (and therefore my) dreams and goals. For instance, he was tall, and I am short. I did not yet understand that my happiness would come from setting and achieving my own goals. Period.

Unfortunately, his stressful lifestyle included the then-popular three martini lunches. This almost daily structure in his business led him deep into alcoholism. As I saw my brother stripped down by that disease, the shock caused many conflicting thoughts in my mind. At first, I denied it. Finally, I realized his failures, and I began to choose for myself what his life meant to me as I formulated my own.

Eventually and especially with the help of my first wife, Lori, my own self-talk evolved. I began to realize I could learn from my brother in ways other than just trying to imitate him. I saw for the first time that I was not, never could be, and actually didn't *want* to be him. He had given me the gift of going before and letting me see his life unfold. My experiences, and especially talks with Lori, made me realize I was better off to be a very different, self-defined person. I still loved my brother just as much; I respected his skills and loved the sober version of him. But apparently, he did not and hid in the disease.

Right after my first cancer was found and I underwent that rapid, massive surgery, my brother came to visit us, supposedly to help. He had ideas of driving my kids to school and helping Lori around the house while I was totally incapacitated. But he must have been feeling inadequate (negative self-talk) in his effort to deal with my cancer-wracked state and appearance. The addiction reared its head. The first morning, he quickly got drunk on his morning orange juice. He had spiked it with shot after shot of vodka from my bar (secretly, he thought), and he abused Lori the rest of the day. This was the final turning point for me. My evolving positive self-talk shouted at me to pull away from him, not as a brother, but only as a model and idol.

We can't hide from our self-talk. As I said, it is us. Imagine my brother's self-talk in trying to deal with the pressure of that high-powered career. He may not have even known he was trying to hide from negative self-talk by getting caught up in self-medicating that mental pain. His medication was alcohol combined with an addictive personality. I cringe at the thought of his poor self-talk. He must have been so tough on himself inside. Over a period of years, he began losing great jobs, not because his great performance was slipping but because of his verbal abusiveness to others when under the influence. He lost two wives and families and friends— and eventually, his own life—because of alcoholism.

He lived a paradox. He had so much and yet enjoyed so little. I can only imagine his self-talk and how much damage he let it inflict on him. He didn't know he had a choice.

On a summer morning, stone-cold sober, but exhausted and recovering from a physically weakening three-day bender, Bob tripped at the top of a steep set of stone steps that went down to street level from the high perch of his beautiful Golden Gate-view house in San Francisco.

Three days later, my sister and I were at Bob's hospital bedside conferring with the doctors. My brother died that day, but he had given me yet another lifelong and lifesaving gift. I knew I had some of my brother's addictive traits. From then on, he has been a source of strength and not sadness for me because of what I choose to view as his final gift:

exposure to the destruction of a life by addiction. I have veered away from his disease and addictive behavior, even though I have come perilously close in times of confusion and weakness. He has inspired a large part of my saving self-talk to this day.

Here's a final comparative for you to consider as I try to convey to you the power of managing your self-talk. Not doing so is like a person with significant sleep apnea refusing to wear a CPAP device at night. Both will experience a diminished quality of life. The lack of a CPAP reduces oxygen to the brain and destroys brain cells. The proliferation of negative self-talk destroys opportunities and even peace of mind. (And yes, I do wear a CPAP every night.)

CHAPTER 3

RESET EQUALS RENEWAL

The measure of a man is the way he bears up under misfortune.

—Plutarch

Git'er done!

—Larry the Cable Guy

For me, the word *reset* means reestablishing positive self-talk wherever and whenever circumstances significantly change to impede my effort to achieve a goal, large or small. It is my means of realigning my self-talk with new, usually unexpected circumstances. My version of *reset* is the ultimate method of adaptability to get back to a productive, achieving mentality quickly.

Reset = renewed determination

If I go "underwater" emotionally for a moment, I have learned to check myself and engage my self-talk to help me recover quickly to keep going. Keep on keepin' on.

The concept of reset works hand-in-hand with self-talk, which you now know I view as a very powerful force in our lives. It is with us every minute we are awake. How we manage and respond to it has far-reaching consequences in the short and long term in every experience of our lives. We must see the opportunities to make the most of our lives and those of our loved ones by adapting to new circumstances.

Back on Track

A few years ago my wife, Olivia, and I were staying in a lovely bed and breakfast in the Garden District in New Orleans. It is a 110-year-old house that at once is charming and maddening for the owner and her visitors. The owner was obviously getting fed up with some things. We noted during our stay that these annoyances would occasionally but only temporarily overwhelm her long-term love of the charming house. Maybe the most common thing was that she was constantly called into the breakfast room by guests who were blowing out an electric circuit by running both the toaster and toaster-oven simultaneously. As we were chatting with her after breakfast one morning about her lovely home and this frequent event, she said offhand, "At least I can reset the circuit immediately and we're back on track." That got me thinking about the word *reset*.

Have you ever watched a beginning kayaker in the waves on a beach in the ocean? Have you ever seen kayakers in competition, say in the Olympics? Beginning kayakers flip over—a lot. They are taught to flip themselves right back up without panicking. Great kayakers have learned to flip right back up within a second or two to keep on course and keep winning (achieving goals). That's what the reset does for me mentally and emotionally. If I go "underwater" emotionally for a moment, I have taught myself to be aware that I am upside-down. With that awareness, I check my self-talk, flip right side up quickly, and keep on keepin' on with a better outlook and attitude right then and there.

As you have read already in this book, I believe achieving and maintaining a positive attitude can be learned, not just inherited. I also believe you can reshape your attitude at any time in your life. I have trouble believing some of us are born with a so-called happy gene. Alternatively, we are not born to be eternally sad or grouchy people either. Becoming aware of the quality of our self-talk is our responsibility and is a critical step in the (re)training of our mind. To be truthful, I stand here as proof. Ask my wife. I can be a grouchy guy, but I have learned how to "straighten up and fly right." My dad was a gentle man, but there were times he was not afraid to be a father. I hear his voice from long ago telling me to do just that. More times than I care to remember, he would look at me and sternly say,

"Straighten up and fly right, son!" When I acted up, that's the next thing I heard. I knew what he meant, and I knew he meant it.

Today, even though I might have some grouchy moments around home, in public, I am almost always a happy person known for looking on the bright side or "being a diplomat." Since other people believe that, I have a tendency to prove them right. That means positive self-talk is always my way of thinking. That might be part of the reason behind my moderately successful career. My point is that it's important both personally and professionally to manage your self-talk.

It really is possible to begin catching yourself as you veer into negativity. I maintain that you can reset yourself or get back on a positive track, just as the kayakers flip themselves from underwater. From my experience, it is a skill that only gets better with practice. As you begin working with your self-talk, you will become sensitive to attitude triggers. They will alert you when you slip off track. This reset idea then directly intervenes to enable you to manage your self-talk.

When I go to the grocery store, I'm bored. It's an assignment. I am not a foodie, though I enjoy a great meal at home or in a wonderful restaurant. I just would prefer that someone else shop for and prepare it. Maybe I have dog in my ancestry, because I would rather have it set down before me than have the pride of having prepared it. Anyway, when I have finished the list my wife gave me, it always seems to be the moment when you hear over the intercom, "Jonas, please open register four," because the lines have just lengthened by a factor of three. I growl to myself, as I know I will be stuck in the store for a lot longer.

Here's my moment of reset. I use my self-talk. Here's a key word you will see again and again as you read: *choose*. I choose to look at the most attractive, eye-pleasing thing in the store while I have to wait in the line. That immediately changes my focus from the long line to something nice. Yep, nine times out of ten, it is the woman three people ahead of me or in the next line over. I'm a guy! But sometimes, it's the beautiful flowers out for Mother's Day or a great photo on a magazine cover. Reality check! Why should I grumble about how long the lines are when I can't change the line but I can change my self-talk and enjoy the totality of my surroundings? *Come on, Dave, reset.* Give yourself (and others who have to live with you) a break!

Maya Angelou, wonderful writer and poet and Pulitzer Prize nominee, once said, "If you don't like something, change it. If you can't change it, change your attitude."

There are diamonds at our feet all the time. We can coach ourselves through our self-talk to look around and find something to enjoy rather than to grumble about. There's truth to the old saying, "Laugh and the world laughs with you. Cry and you cry alone." Please try this simple exercise the next time you are in a long line in a store, at the airport, in a traffic jam, or any other place that slows you down from your normal pace. Choose to enjoy the moment you've been given rather than fight it and let it upset you. It's simple but not easy. But you can do it if I can. In these everyday experiences, we are no different from each other. Choose to enjoy rather than struggle through your life. Your choice.

Sleep Well?

Here's a different example of resetting that my wife and I experienced. I came into the kitchen one morning and asked her the question most of us ask our partners in the morning. I asked if she slept well. She took my question seriously as she responded with feeling, "Actually, not well at all." Her voice was full of weariness. Unfortunately, she sometimes gets into what she describes as a "broken record" of worrying thoughts during the night.

Understanding that as a real answer, I wanted to help her, just as she is always helping me during my cancer treatments and other medical events. Trying to be empathetic, I suggested, "Here is an opportunity to use another version of the reset concept." I told her to change the subject. "What?" she asked, thinking I meant right now. "No, no," I said with a cautious smile.

I decided to use an example to explain. She might think of the fantastic good times we had on a recent trip or a great time at someone's party or recall the pure, low-key enjoyment of just talking with a good friend during her morning walks. She has a great sense of humor. She lives with me; she has to. I suggested she use it. "Tell yourself a joke. Really."

I saw her skeptical, you-don't-understand look, so I said, "Try it next time, please. You may find yourself smiling at the ceiling rather than frowning at a wall as you put your feet on the floor in the morning. If you start doing any of these things, you are, by definition, self-talk resetting and blocking out the negatives." I explained it takes practice, like any skill. And you have to want to do it. To learn to ride a bike, we go through quite a few times of failure, but we really want to and we've seen others do it, so we keep trying, and voila! We learn to ride.

Next time you can't fall asleep because of anxiety, give this next version of my reset a try. I was worrying about something one weekend and I couldn't even change the subject, as I had just suggested to my wife. So I chose a more drastic method. I got up five times to write what I was thinking down on a pad of paper I keep in the bathroom. I kept getting up until it was gone. It's crazy, but when I dump the thought out on paper, the worry diminishes. That's another version of nighttime reset. I know I can deal with it tomorrow, so for now, it is gone when I get back in bed. I have reduced the fear of forgetting it and realized I can deal with it tomorrow better than tonight. Again, like riding a bike, first you have to try. But then you'll only need to learn it once—and then keep doing it until you are really good at it and can count on it. This technique will get easier and more comforting with each effort.

When it comes to cancer, I am the one who has had it, so I know what it feels like. But Olivia, as my true love and caregiver all wrapped in one, does not really know how it feels or how I feel moment to moment. I should explain something here. An analogy that applies to our relationship during cancer episodes would have my body being the driver of an almost-out-of-control car and Olivia as a passenger. As you know, when you drive a car, the driver thinks he "knows" where he is going next and calmly sees the curve ahead. But a nervous passenger has no way to be sure and may want to say, "There's a curve ahead. Aren't we going too fast?" During my cancer times, I think Olivia has felt as the passenger would and worries through the night while I, the sick guy, get to sleep soundly.

No matter how well she knows me, cancer is a different game. I know she fears the day I am not here—what she will do, where she will go. The nights are tough on the cancer carrier, but I wonder if they are not even tougher, at times, on the caregiver. Also, in our case, Olivia is the detail person. When we've been in cancer mode, details of our process and progress fly through her mind constantly. For me, even though I'm the patient, not so much. It is my nature to focus on the process of getting well more than the facts and statistics and names of medicines and when to take them.

Triggers

A few years back, during my most recent and most serious run-in with cancer, Olivia began letting me know that I was not being myself more and more frequently. My normally good humor had disappeared. This was not without justification, as several doctors in our search had told us I was inoperable, and simultaneously, I was taking the worst form of chemotherapy. I'm not a big guy to start with, and my weight had dropped from around 160 pounds to around 125 pounds. I won't digress further by explaining all the issues; they're not important to my point, and those of us around cancer and chemo know the side effects without my expanding on them. Let's just say the side effects were getting bigger and I was getting smaller. It seemed my cancer was in control rather than me.

Olivia and I realized I was developing an attitude problem that was showing up in our relationship and even in communication with my friends. This was a medically induced situation rather than the normal Dave-type grouchiness I occasionally dealt with before chemo. This was a new dimension. She's a smart lady, and I care about her opinions, so her comment sensitized me, even though I didn't like the news at the time. In fact, I angrily denied her accusation that I was assuming an attitude. Perfect! I had thereby denied and proved her point all in one moment. Nice going, grouch.

As I took her comment to heart, I began to realize a couple of words and feelings that seemed to be there each time I began slipping into anger and negativity. We talked about it and decided this might be an opportunity for us to implement my reset concept: here comes water, flip the kayak. I have a tendency for teaming up, and this came into play, too. As I explored this with Olivia, she noticed that there were key words or categories in conversations that we could look for to indicate I was fading.

When we became aware of these triggers and I began to feel upset, I excused myself and left that room for a moment, company or not. If we were in a restaurant, I would go to the restroom and get some distance from whatever or whoever was upsetting me.

Once I was away from that immediate environment—a scientist might call it "the stimulus"—it became easier for me to identify and set the issue aside without having to resolve it then and there. Having identified the issue, I could go back with this new awareness and speak up calmly about it or delicately and consistently change the subject, thereby diffusing the issue. I was managing my self-talk and my environment rather than reacting to it with emotions of anger or fear. In other words, I was able to reset myself and quickly become free to be a happy participant in the original environment rather than fighting my way to the end of the evening.

I found this amazingly effective. Eventually, I even told my wife some of the triggers (like politics) so she could help me to reset even sooner and without having to leave the table or room. Warning: those kicks under the table can be painful. The times I used or heard a trigger word occurred more often than I had expected, and frequently, I was not aware, while Olivia was. So we created a key word she could say to me: *Grace.* This was much better than her kicking me under the table. She would look directly at my eyes and softly say, "Grace" to indicate I was acting poorly. I would be the only one who would know what it meant or why she had said it. I would simply say thanks to indicate I had received the message, and I still do, because we use it to this day. I would reset: "straighten up and fly right, son!" or "flip my kayak" accordingly.

Defining Grace

Why the word *grace*? First of all, there are religious definitions of grace. Then there is the simple nonreligious definition of moving effortlessly (e.g., she swam *gracefully* through the water.)

But neither of these is my exact thought. I define *grace* simply as being mindful of my thankfulness for the goodness in my life, regardless of what might be upsetting or even dire circumstances at the time. And if times are good, I hope to be humble regardless of how good my situation may be.

Our definition and use of the word came from something I told Olivia as tears welled up during chemotherapy after we had been told several times surgery was not a possibility. We had been to three cancer centers and interviewed five doctors. We knew I was in deep trouble. One day, I said, "You know, Olivia, if these are my final days, I want to live them with grace." To this day, it remains a powerful guiding word for me, whether she says it or I think it. Cancer or not, it represents a way of life, of being, to which I aspire to live the rest of my life. I can't choose how long my life might be. The way I act during my life, I can choose.

Jenny Acting Up and the "Reset"

Long ago, I would have perceived *reset* as a kind of negative phrase, like *attitude control*, because I had not had the experience at the bed and breakfast in New Orleans or the humbling experience of cancer. Even so, it was a valid approach that I came upon naturally when raising my two kids. Here's how it unfolded with our first child, Jenny.

One evening years ago, when we had friends over, my first child and dear daughter, Jenny, was in the living room with the adults; my wife, Lori, was in the kitchen. Now in her thirties, Jenny was then about six years old. While we adults were having a great time, Jenny was feeling a little left out and wanted more attention. Suddenly, I heard a small crash. Nothing broke, but the bowl of assorted nuts we had put out had mysteriously flown off the coffee table, and nuts were all over the floor. Jenny was doing what all kids do. Lacking attention, she chose a negative way of gaining it and decided to cause a ruckus. The nuts on the floor were part of it. This was obviously unpleasant for her mom, who came quickly into the room, and me, as well as for our guests. We became more uncomfortable as she became defiant about the mess. Out of the box, I reacted with a bark of her name, "Jenny!" Uh-oh. I had reacted emotionally with my own feelings rather than thinking where we all wanted this to end up. Perfect. She had me. Jenny faded toward tears. And inside, I was saying to myself, *Now I've validated her negative actions with my anger and negative attention. How do I recover?*

I remember settling myself and asking Jenny to come to me. I calmed down and touched her gently and said, "Jenny, I have a project for you." She peeked up at me. "Would you please go to your bedroom and stay in there until you can smile again?" I continued, "Everyone here in this room was smiling before you spilled those nuts. Mom's picking them up now, so don't worry about that. Let me take you to your room, and as soon as you can find that smile, come back out and smile with the happy people again. Okay?" Slowly, the little blonde head with the frown nodded. She wouldn't—or couldn't—look up at me, but she then turned toward her room before I could take her hand, and she accepted my challenge. Her head down, she quickly departed down the hall toward her room.

Of course, it didn't take her long. When she reappeared with a big smile, we all cheered and celebrated her finding her smile. And I smiled back at her as I said, "We have a happy girl again." She was now getting attention for a good reason rather than a negative one. Perfect. She was my little angel again.

Funny, in a way, she learned managing self-talk and reset before I did.

CHAPTER 4

WHATEVER IS, IS RIGHT

> Man knows so little. We are not the architects of our
> existence. We must wait to judge the meaning and the
> value of events in our lives.
> —Alexander Pope, from "An Essay on Man," 1734

Ever read the classic children's story "Dumbo"? I can remember my mom reading it to me at bedtime when I was just a little tyke, four or five years old. I've always loved the story because of the message the author conveys to the reader. In fact, I read "Dumbo" to Jenny's daughter, a.k.a. my granddaughter, Lucy, as one of her bedtime stories. We try to pass the wisdom on, right? It is a story of fear overcome by using a feather. We can all identify our feather, just like Dumbo did.

Dumbo is a small elephant with very big ears. Those two challenges prevent him from joining his mother and the other elephants in the circus show. His little mouse friend, Timothy, encourages him to try to fly during his part in a lowly clown act because his outsized ears are big enough to act as wings, but Dumbo doesn't believe he can. Convinced that Dumbo can fly, Timothy Mouse encourages Dumbo by telling him that holding a crow's feather in his trunk will enable him to fly. They climb up to the high wire and jump during the clown act. In the air, as his ears open, Dumbo begins gliding but loses the feather. After a scary moment, he finds he really can fly, just as the mouse had told him he could. Timothy Mouse becomes

Dumbo's manager, and the ringmaster quickly promotes Dumbo and his mother to stars of the show.

Why have I just told you a children's story? Because Dumbo overcomes his fear and uses it to empower himself. He is persuaded by Timothy to use a prop to get him off the ground (pun intended). By doing so, he realizes he can overcome the fear he feels. Once he has removed the fear, he overcomes the obstacles that were preventing him from experiencing the good in his life.

As I said, this story had the effect on me that my mom intended. I began to understand I had to believe in myself to accomplish things, even if I had to find a feather to get started. Years later, in high school, I found just such a feather. It is a phrase in a poem that I turned into a lifetime aphorism.

My Feather

Here is how I found my feather. One night during my junior year in high school, I was reading my English literature homework assignment. My main objective was to finish it and move on to more interesting things. Or maybe I just wanted to finish studying and go downstairs to be with my dad and stepmom, Casey. Either way, I was not motivated to read stilted eighteenth-century literature that night. Pushing myself to focus for just a while longer before quitting, I began reading the assignment.

It was called "An Essay on Man" by Alexander Pope. He wrote it in 1734. It was long, and as it turned out, I never made it downstairs. I stayed up late that night, but not because of the essay's length. It mesmerized me with its message. This work states, in essence, that we have no idea of the grand scheme of things. We look only at events in our lives and around us and attempt to make sense of them from our limited perspective.

It is said that this essay, more than any other work at that time in England and Europe, popularized an optimistic philosophy. It is a rationalistic effort to justify to humanity the over-arching ways of godly philosophy. As is typical of me, I eventually identified one sentence in the work that seemed to be the heart of Pope's message, and I memorized it so I could carry the thought with me, in the same way Dumbo carried his feather. I came to a paragraph written in the arcane eighteenth-century English I was struggling to understand and stared at it. I read and reread it several times. I ask you to do the same.

All nature is but art, unknown to thee;
All chance, direction, which thou canst not see,
All discord, harmony not understood;
All partial evil, universal good:
And spite of pride, in erring reason's spite,
One truth is clear, Whatever is, is right.

Then I focused on an abbreviation of the last paragraph above and created a single line: "All partial evil, universal good." And then, "Whatever is, is right."

What does Pope mean by that? Kids in today's world might say, "It's all good." Little do they know how accurate it is or how much power is in that phrase. I simplistically deciphered Pope's arcane version of "It's all good" as I read and reread the entire work that night.

My interpretation, while fuzzy that night, became clearer in time with use of my new aphorism. First of all, I see that Pope is encouraging us, emphasis on the core word *courage*. If we will persevere when bad things surround us, the good in this world will always reappear, given one's patience. This aphorism from the essay had a major impact on my attitude back then. Most importantly, it buoyed my faith as I thought about it and applied it as a template to gauge events over the next ten years and, frankly, for the rest of my life. It became my feather.

Pope's thought seemed to say to me back then, "Life makes sense, son. You just can't see it from your current limited perspective. Patience. Give it time." That archaic phrase became a mantra of reassurance to me in times of tribulation. It was especially helpful to me when an event made no sense at the time of its occurrence. There I was, sixteen years old, and my perspective was that of a wounded bird just beginning to really fly again.

One of the "partial evil" events was that I had tragically lost my forty-six-year-old mom to cancer when I was eleven; then things got worse as I experienced three years of a directionless, vandalism-ridden, moping, "latchkey" existence. But the universal part of the goodness of life came roaring back to me at age thirteen. My father married Casey (below).

My stepmom arrived, and our relationship launched me in a wondrous new and productive direction. This wounded bird was taking flight again. It was, for me, a miracle. As I sat there that night, a young kid struggling with the philosophical meaning of this essay, was I living Pope's thoughts?

Wow. From my brightened new perspective with Casey in our lives, life really was wonderful again. More later about her and how our time together forever shaped my outlook and attitude during the next three years. For now, suffice it to say I was, with her insight and assistance, building an outlook that would help me cope with my cancer experiences in later years. The good had resurfaced. My "feather" came to me in this essay. It professed an enduring thought for me. My faith began to take shape.

The bad things in life inevitably lead to the good, given patience and my enduring search. As I moved through my life, what seemed so horrific then, given more time, had turned out so wonderfully. But another "partial evil" event was not far away. The next summer, between my junior and senior years, I lost my dad to a massive stroke. He was fifty-six, and he was gone in three days.

Newspaper clippings used by permission of The Times Union

Imagine the challenge to the way I had found to gird myself emotionally and mentally after having lost my mom. I lost two parents by age sixteen. How could this turn out to be good? But patience, Pope counsels at another part of the essay: "Man knows so little. We are not the architects of our existence. We must wait to judge the meaning and the value of events in our lives."

Eventually, I understood what he was saying, but this was an incredibly difficult thing to do. This is not the version of patience we exercise while waiting for a stoplight or for a bus. Pope was encouraging me to have patience with my life and the unpredictable events that suddenly send us caroming off in a different direction. Moreover, he is encouraging his reader to have that patience consistently over a lifetime. Pope says this without providing a value judgment. That's part of his point. From a bad occurrence, the optimistic person who uses positive self-talk will, by definition, find a way back to the good in whatever new paradigm he finds himself, however long it takes. Expect the best, and over time, you will be amazed.

Faith

The point is that Pope's words impacted my faith. With his words, I found I could regain and eventually maintain my perspective as events, both positive and negative, unfolded in front of me and impacted my life. I would self-talk the thought, *Be patient - all partial evil, universal good. Have faith. Look for the good.* Just as things seemed to be crashing around me again with my father's death, that phrase steadied me.

You may have experienced a moment when you have said to yourself, "Oh, my, things are just going too well. I'd better watch my back!" I'll wager that you self-talk that phrase twice as often as some version of "Phooey, things are going so poorly. I'm sure they'll turn around." Pope was saying to me that night that even though horrific things may happen, we shouldn't give in to the evil. Don't give up. Never give up. Keep your faith. Keep on keepin' on, and keep looking for the good in the world. Seek it. Expect it, and you will find it.

Determination

With that kind of faith comes determination. Starting when I was forty-two, my cancer came and went four times. As I move past my seventieth birthday, who knows, it may return yet another time. But I choose—I determine—to embrace my cancer as part of my life. I have never expected anything other than the best outcomes. Yes, I've had the momentary losses of faith that we all have, and that has been when my self-talk and reset have come in. We just cannot let pessimism overwhelm the good in life.

I have trusted that I could find the best outcome in any situation. I had done that with each of my parents' deaths. I have found that when bad things happen, my best response is to doggedly seek to reset my self-talk. I know my best choice in life is to return as quickly as possible to expect and actively seek the best outcome—the good in life. Forming that habit of restoring my faith through self-talk has been, and is to this day, critical to my well-being and my survival.

The White Room

Speaking of seeking the good when all seems to be crashing down around us, I recently had to relive one of those moments. I was talking with my fifty-something-year-old niece, Melinda, and mentioned the way I visualized the quandary in which Olivia and I found ourselves in 2010 when my most recent cancer challenge occurred. While shaken by yet another bout with the disease and a lack of confidence in some local oncologists, we immediately thought of the last successful surgery in 1998 and the excellent doctor who had performed it.

He was in Houston at M. D. Anderson, and his name was Dr. Jeffrey Lee. He had done the marvelous complicated surgery to remove my right kidney, surrounding tissue, and tumor in 1998. We felt certain he would say, "Sorry to hear you're up against it again, Dave. Sure, sign these papers and we will set up for the surgery in a month or so."

Dr. Lee is a kind and capable man. So when he came into the exam room with MRI in hand and told us he wanted to show us why he would not operate this time, we were devastated. The cancer was far too widespread. We were shocked as wave after wave of bad news hit us. It had attached to and possibly invaded half of my liver and spiraled up my vena cava. From there, it was claiming the right side of my diaphragm and looked as if it might eventually threaten my heart.

We had assumed he would say yes to surgery. How wrong we were. He told us I should take four months of intensely powerful chemo to see if we could reduce the size of the tumor to an operable level. The last studies on my type of cancer were from the 1990s in Italy with a pitifully small sample, but he said the chemotherapy regimen was our only choice. We pleaded that he reconsider, but he was resolute. Crushed, we accepted his referral to a research oncologist in the same cancer center.

I told Melinda the old saying, "Never assume anything" came to mind later that day as we contemplated four months of body-wracking chemo as our "only choice," to quote Dr. Lee.

I remember that days later, as Olivia and I flew back from Houston to San Diego, we talked through soft tears. I remember saying to Olivia, "Okay, they say they can't operate, but at least they could be truthful about how long they think I have. They won't even say that. They just say take the chemotherapy and we'll see." Yes, that was a very low point with lots of negative self-talk raging. I was just sitting there starting to feel sorry for myself. Was my motto, "I will die with this cancer, not from it," really not true?

I told Melinda, in a way, that moment was worse than hearing I had cancer the first time back in 1986. Back then, I hardly knew what cancer was, other than it was really bad. My mom had died from it, and some acquaintances had dealt with it. When I was told I had cancer in 1986, I hardly had time to build a reaction beyond shock, as I was on an operating table within days. This fourth time of hearing those words, "You have cancer again," was different. I now knew the true threat and many trials I was facing. I (we) knew just how difficult our immediate future would be and could be, even if I survived. What if Dr. Lee was right? What if surgery was not an option this time?

I took a breath to gain a bit more composure from visualizing that moment. Smiling gently, Melinda asked me to go on. I told her we immediately scheduled another round-trip flight to Houston. This trip was specifically to start the chemotherapy treatment after our talk with Dr. Lee. I sat or lay in a bed for the better part of three or four days. Each day was a six- to eight-hour stretch of receiving poison into my body. Sweet Olivia bought me the original version of an iPad to use during those sessions to try to give me something to do. Then we flew home and I began taking an ever-increasing number of toxic chemo pills each day, starting with five and ending four months later with thirteen to fifteen pills a day. I was consistently poisoning myself with ever more lethal doses of a derivative of

DDT. The days of chemo injections in Houston continued every month, and inevitably, the pounds fell off and the hair fell out.

I related to Melinda how we felt heading home from the airport after the first visit for chemotherapy. Dr. Lee had said that devastating *no* to surgery. Then, to reinforce the shock of that negative news, our talk with the oncologist had been unsettling rather than reassuring. As Olivia and I talked on the plane home after my first round of chemotherapy, my better self-talk began resetting by visualizing us as being in a white room. It was big, and we were the only things in it. The ceiling and the floor and the walls were pure antiseptic white. I imagined the question we were asking ourselves over and over was: "How do we get out?" I could "see" we were sitting there in the middle of that room, just as I had been sitting in those injection rooms. Now we were sitting in the airplane, and the question had changed insidiously from wondering how we would get out to wondering how long I had to live. Ah, I suddenly realized we had evolved to the wrong question! Worrying about something I can't change won't solve things.

Continuing our conversation in the car in San Diego, still staring at those same "white walls" in my mind, we began thinking and acting positively to resolve things. Contrary to my status in those chemo rooms, I realized that in the rooms in my mind, we could choose not to just sit there. It looked futile, but we must make the effort. In my mind, we stood up and began feeling the white walls as high as we could reach. We walked every inch of the white floor looking for some hint of a way out. We stared intently at the white, seamless ceiling looking for any clue.

From that car ride home, we never gave up or lost heart again for more than a moment. What good would sitting and feeling sorry for ourselves do? We knew we could, had to, take action, just as in my visualization. To be frank, even if I had died, Olivia would remember me as her partner who did everything he could, not as one who would just sit and wait to die in that white room.

Melinda smiled as I came out of reliving that moment and I completed the story of my visualization with what she knew had happened next.

The research oncologist we were referred to in Houston turned into another part of the problem: "challenge," my self-talk says. We were flying down to see her and get continuing injection treatments. But one of those times, she left us in one of her waiting rooms for more than two hours.

When we asked the nurse who had been reassuring us the doctor would be with us "shortly," she became flustered and admitted the doctor had run out to catch a plane to make an out-of-town presentation the next day. What? How could she have done that? Could we at least talk to her by phone if she was not yet on the plane? No. Obviously we were devastated. I took the chemo the next two days, and we flew home.

The more we thought about it, the more furious we were at the thoughtless way we had been treated. We decided once again to take action. We asked that all oncology services be performed by an oncologist at a local hospital so we did not have to travel anymore or receive such poor delivery of services but could still be linked to Dr. Lee's offices.

To achieve this local service, we asked many friends for referrals to oncologists in San Diego. We didn't realize it at the time, but this was a very unusual request. Oncologists don't usually perform services prescribed by another oncologist from another hospital. They like to prescribe and administer chemo and do reviews themselves. I think they feel there is risk to an arrangement such as the one we were seeking. It looked grim. Then came an amazing turn of events. The good we had been seeking appeared.

We had a breakthrough: we not only found Dr. Fred Millard, a highly capable oncologist who was willing to see us even though we were still technically being served as a patient of the hospital in Houston, but he also turned out to be wonderful person.

After months of searching for and interviewing doctors who might take on my challenge with me, all the while enduring the effects of my ever-increasing doses of chemo, there it was: a little part of one of the white walls finally moved and became a switch that opened up a fantastic opportunity for me. In reality, that "little part" was not so little. This new oncologist not only provided chemo services; he also helped Olivia and me find a team of surgeons willing to strap on their gowns and try to save my life at the University of California, San Diego—yes, a hospital right in my hometown. The white walls fell away for Olivia and me. Dumbo would say, "I knew you could fly." Pope would smile and say, "You have once again been patient and persistent enough to find the 'good' in your life."

You may have those times when the white walls and ceiling and floor seem to surround you. No way out, you say? From my experience, Pope's version of patience does not include sitting and waiting. I implore you to look for the good in life. But be patient on your way to being fearless. Keep resetting and replacing your self-talk with, "There is always a way out," and reach for the good. It may come in a strange form different from mine, but it will be there. Never, never give up. Grace!

My new doctor, or as some would say, "my new best friend," helped me complete my chemo and transfer all my medical records and introduced me to a surgeon who then put together a team of six, including heart and liver specialists. It was what some doctors call "heroic surgery" with very high risks. After eight hours, Olivia rose to her feet in the waiting room as she watched Dr. Andrew Lowy, the lead surgeon who had put the team together, come toward her. He had a tired but broad smile. She knew before he spoke what he was going to say and smiled back at him. Six days later, I awakened in the ICU to the rest of my life. Once again, I was back on track to my goal to die with this cancer rather than from it.

CHAPTER 5

T'AI CHI TO MY CHI

Never miss a good chance to shut up.

—Will Rogers

Nothing under heaven is softer or more yielding than water; but when it attacks things hard and resistant, there is nothing that can withstand it. That the yielding conquers the resistant and the soft conquers the hard is a fact known by all men, yet utilized by none.

—Lao Tzu, "Tao Te Ching"

Well, Maybe by One

What would you think if I were to tell you that I can overcome a challenge by surrendering? I think you might say in your self-talk, "Is he kidding asking me that question?" No, I am not. It is just counterintuitive. Let me explain by saying it's all about t'ai chi. Oh dear, that didn't help, did it? Well, let me give you a story or two to clarify.

First the concept: like the words *self-talk* and *reset*, you may have heard references to t'ai chi, an ancient Eastern style of fighting, but you don't know why I am directing you to it now. And what is t'ai chi, anyway? First of all, in Chinese, the word *chi* means "life force" or "life energy" or "spirit." The full name, "t'ai chi chuan," translates roughly to "grand ultimate fist." T'ai chi is a thoughtful, artful, and effective form of initially defensive physical combat. A key part of the strategy involved in this martial arts style is avoiding direct confrontation and yet putting yourself in a position of using the opponent's energy to eventually win the struggle. It is essentially counterintuitive in that it applies calm against action, slow against fast, and soft against hard. China has been the home of and heart of this martial art (also turned art form) since the twelfth century.

Let's imagine a punch is thrown at you by an aggressor. In its simplest terms, instead of raising your arm or hand to block the punch, which is the intuitive response, you step aside and cause the punch to only graze or even miss you. You move to the side or back away, i.e., "surrender" by creating an empty space. The force of the thrown punch hitting only air will cause the aggressor's body to follow in the direction of his punch, causing him to be off balance. Suddenly, he is reeling past you or at least is way off balance. You have now "surrendered" to a stronger or superior position, with the aggressor off balance or on the ground. You now have control of the situation through the power of his energy. Some t'ai chi experts actually are able to grab the opponent's flying wrist and pull the aggressor in the direction of his punch. When this happens, the expert, using a minimal amount of his strength, causes the aggressor to go flying in the direction of his punch to the ground, and the expert stands above him, now in control of the match.

The site www.Taichimania.com describes the result of this physical move this way: "The t'ai chi classics describe this level of skill as 'deflecting a thousand-pound momentum with a trigger force of four ounces.'"

My Chi

I have given you this description of physical t'ai chi because I have learned to take the physical principles and convert them into what is effectively mental and social t'ai chi. I call it "My Chi." I know I am asking you to take a mental leap for a moment, pun intended. I ask you to accept that I have converted the physical version of t'ai chi to steps of strategic thinking I use whether I am involved in self-talk, in a discussion with others, or in a longer-term social situation where I have a desire to influence the outcome without or with minimal confrontation.

My version of t'ai chi, My Chi, is a method of thinking, expressing my thoughts, and negotiating to accomplish my goals as I encounter other people and deal with them along the way. And as you learn more about My Chi, you will see that my entire concept of not fighting my cancer, but instead empowering myself by "embracing" it and making it a part of me, is based on My Chi.

Cynics can call it mental gymnastics, but rather than fighting my cancer, I chose to mentally recognize and accept it was attacking me. Then, rather than fight it, I chose to mentally step aside, not out of fear but instead as part of a strategy. My surrender is not flight caused by fright. My thought during my cancer experiences was that my cancer is me, so I now own it. If I own it, with the right effort, I can control it. By accepting it and adapting to it, I now have gained a stronger mental position from which to deal with my cancer.

In effect, cancer was throwing punches at me. Rather than blocking them with rising anger and fear, I accepted and embraced my cancer. Rather than fearing it, I became calmer and felt more in control. I achieved a peace of mind with which to go forward. For me, peace of mind was not possible initially, when I was fighting with something I feared.

In the social world, when a person seems to represent an obstacle or challenge to one of my goals, in effect throwing a verbal punch at me, I have learned to avoid directly contradicting them. I accept and invite them into further discussion. By engaging them and encouraging further discussion, I am able to continue our interaction and eventually provide guidance and information about my views on the subject from strength (a "superior position") to achieve my goal. Importantly, this assumes my idea is valid and the other person's statement or belief is in error, much as he initially might believe it to be true.

What if I am wrong? If, in fact, he is right and I am wrong, this is not a bad outcome. I then benefit from learning something. I am not afraid to be wrong with My Chi. I may have been corrected, so to speak, but I benefit in a different way than being right. I learn and I am saved from making a mistake. It is a win for us both as My Chi unfolds in a dialogue rather than in an argument.

I have used My Chi widely. Most importantly, my approach to both the disease itself and to those with whom I have dealt to become well again are paramount, but I also have broadened my use of My Chi into other parts of my life with consistent success.

We Have a Choice

It is not always obvious, but these principles hold in many situations. When someone throws a psychological or conversational challenge at you, what is your immediate reaction, your intuitive response? For most of us, it's generally an oral version of either fight or flight. You throw up your verbal arms to block the person's verbal fist from contacting you, right? You fend off the blow and either try to counterpunch by introducing your opposing thought directly (fight) or accept his thought as correct (even though you really don't agree with the contender's thought) just to get away (flight). You are now irritated that you lost control of the discussion and maybe lost the discussion point as well, even though you continue to believe you are still right and he is wrong. No one benefits from this outcome.

But what about a third choice, not intuitive or instinctive? What if you accept, without validating, the contender's comment, thereby surrendering for the moment only that his thought has been heard? You can use patience and a nonjudgmental comment such as, "Interesting," or, "Tell me more." As he continues, his verbal punch flies past you. He has engaged you—he thinks—and may even think he has the upper hand. Further informed about his challenge, you now have the moment to introduce your thoughtful response rather than having reacted too quickly to his. Fight or flight—yes, those are the instinctive or intuitive responses, but given the conscious, patient effort of listening, you are only surrendering a point by hearing it out. You now set yourself up to win the moment. Again, I am assuming here your point is a valid one.

Now Back to Our Sponsor for This Idea: Cancer

Fending off a blow can be an automatic or intuitive first response with the onset of cancer, too. I know because that's the first thing I did when the doctors told me, "You have a large tumor in your abdomen," back in

1986. Hearing a doctor say, "You have cancer," caused me instinctively to throw up defenses saying, "Oh, no, this can't be." That sounds like the beginning of denial to me.

Or maybe with self-examination, a woman feels a lump in her breast that was not there a month ago. But she self-talks to block the terrible thought by saying to herself, "It is small, probably nothing, a fibroid. I'll keep an eye on it, but I won't mention it to anybody for now." No worries, right? Wrong. Similarly, once your tongue feels a cavity on a molar, you worry, but you don't visit the dentist. If you feel it, trust it. Accept the information. Pull the possibility of cancer or a cavity past you, and gain control by going to the doctor or dentist and doing something. Don't react; act.

My point is there are ways to respond other than directly blocking a blow or running away, the choices of fight or flight. As I look back on my life, I find my choice, My Chi, has been a silver thread stitching together my behavior through many areas and times, whether in my friendships, my career, or especially in my cancer experiences.

Obviously, you now see I don't mean I have gone around using the ancient method of physical battle with my friends, clients, and doctors. I have instead been using the principles of movement and leverage involved in executing the physical t'ai chi to engage my friends, clients, and disease with My Chi mentally and socially to achieve mutually acceptable results with my having a significant hand in the outcome.

Flight or Fight

Isn't an instinctive move what we've always heard is used by most of us in the animal kingdom to respond to sudden threats? It then leads further to fighting or flight. Horses are famous for being animals that always resort to flight. I know this firsthand.

I remember one of the scarier moments in my childhood when my dad and I were spending a sunny day riding horses at a camp near Lake George in upstate New York. My dad was ahead of me. We were just sauntering along and, at seven years old, I was actually becoming a bit bored with just an old trail ride.

Suddenly, there was a noise to the left, just ahead in the bushes along the trail. Holy smoke! My horse wheeled right, steadied up, and then went straight to a gallop the other way, leaving my dad behind me in a fit. Me? I was somehow still on the horse, apoplectic.

As I'm sure you know, a noise or movement of any kind can spook a horse, and this one was spooked and took flight. I now was holding onto the horse, one arm around her neck and the other with a hand full of mane. This gal ignored my rather loud, whiny protestations and took off for the barn. She bolted without investigating whether the noise had been made by a snake, a squirrel, or a salamander.

My real problem developed when this darned horse decided there was a shorter way back to the barn than the trail. This way involved another kind of flight: jumping a small creek. As you might guess, the few moments as we approached the creek were actually more frightening than the brief moment in the air above it. She was in the air, and I was in the air above her for a while. As she landed, I came back down on her hard and barely managed to hang on. I wasn't bored anymore.

Back at the barn, after my dad saw I was safe, he figured he and I had a great story to tell the others when we got back to camp. I didn't want to talk about it. I was embarrassed and sore "you know where." Actually, I think my bruised ego was hurt even more.

Ignoring Is Flight

Is flight the right reaction to solving human problems? I think most of us would say, not usually. Certainly, when dealing with a powerful disease like cancer, flight becomes a very attractive, but in the light of day, maybe not rational, reaction. Self-talk might say, "If I could just get away from this disease ... I'll ignore it." But flight does not deal with the challenge of cancer. It solves nothing. Denial is a form of flight. Initially, you recognize there may be a problem, but rather than deal with it, like the woman during her self-examination, you deny and run from it. In that example, she's avoiding cancer's punch by denying it rather than accepting the information and surrendering to the more powerful position of bringing it to the attention of her doctor. With that choice, she and her doctor can team up and begin to assert control.

Many of us know of people who have had symptoms they should acknowledge as a disease's warning signs, but they deny or run from those symptoms rather than inviting them into their minds to deal with them. It's not just cancer where we react like this. Think heart disease, sleep apnea, infections, and more.

My Chi self-talk says to surrender in a way that you are inviting the symptoms into your mind to deal with them from strength rather than from panic, like my horse. Use your self-talk to accept them rather than fear them. As you invite the possible symptoms of cancer into your mind, you begin to deal with them. Now that you are recognizing them, you can do something about the symptoms. With a visit to a doctor, you may quickly discover there is a tumor, but it is benign. My horse could have stopped and seen it was just a salamander and moved on. But she panicked and bolted at the movement in the bushes.

Acknowledging symptoms early and responding quickly creates the possibility of finding out they are not a bad part of your life. This means you can be done with the worry and move on with your life rather than have a lingering fear. And God forbid, if there is cancer, you can act early with proper treatment and a much higher probability that you walk away a healthy person, rather than a fearful and potentially very sick individual dealing with a maturing version of exactly that which you most feared.

Roar

Horses take flight, but mountain lions are more disposed to stand their ground to fight. We have all heard of runners in parks being attacked along a remote trail. That is the intuitive, instinctive biological response of these beings, especially if it's a mom who has little cubs to feed back at the lair.

In school, we are told to use our intuition and, on an exam, to aggressively choose the first answer we believe is correct and not to change it. Fine for tests; however, for most things in life, we humans can be taught to think differently—counterintuitively, in many cases—and actually achieve more successful outcomes than those achieved by first reactions.

As in the military or in learning to fly a plane, repetitive training builds in the most successful responses to unexpected events to overcome the panic response. But when fending off an unexpected or surprise cancer, there is no repetitive training. To serve ourselves and our families best, we must be able to think on our feet to execute an effective response.

My Chi versus My Cancer

It has been my experience to work toward responding to the onset of cancer not by continuing my first feelings of panicky denial, but instead by consciously choosing to talk myself into a position of control. For me, this began by creating an image of confidence in myself as being more powerful than the cancer through successful self-talk: "It is me; I own it."

I was often able to achieve that feeling or image of calm power, much like sometimes being able to create a feeling of confidence standing over a putt on the golf course. Through My Chi, I found myself in a mental position to offset the panic and more clearly think through my options with my wife and medical advisors. Fear and panic do not serve us well. They have not served me well when I let them rule my mind. And with my cancer, they did at times, but I almost always managed to reset back to that positive outlook of embracing and controlling cancer rather than it controlling me. In time, I found using mental My Chi was the calm place of surrender where my mind is most powerful.

During chemotherapy, I was consistently poisoning myself with ever more lethal doses of chemotherapeutic drugs. When employing t'ai chi, you use the force of your aggressor, so you do not have to feel "strong" to be in control. Even during the mental and physical weakness caused by chemotherapy, I decided I could choose to redirect some negative energy from the debilitating effects of the chemo. Mental energy is energy, so I thought maybe I could positively employ that negative energy to give me strength to overcome the cancer. By doing this mental exercise, I was then in the (mentally) superior position, at least temporarily feeling in control, even though my body was telling me otherwise. Cancer and chemo, the evil twins, the aggressors, were much larger than I am. They were Goliath to my David. We know how the biblical David did. So far, this one, too.

I have used my mental My Chi consistently when I have had my cancer challenges precisely because cancer is much larger and stronger than I am. Accepting cancer and then using its larger power empowers me. If I embrace my cancer and it is part of me, it gives me more power than if I try to fight it. I view fighting as a form of denial, which means I may not even be dealing with the real challenge at hand. Therefore, the image of fighting with or denying cancer was never a solution for me. Denial is a form of fear, and fear can jumble the mind. We all know fear can cause us to do exactly the wrong thing at potentially crucial moments. Fear can cause panic. Whether you are flying an airplane or challenged by cancer, fear and panic are not good resources.

No, rather than fear my cancer, I chose to embrace it. By accepting it as a part of me, it could no longer upset me emotionally. I achieved a clearer, calmer mind and could focus on the issues that mattered with doctors and the administrators, most of whom at times, whether they meant to or not, stood between me and the surgeries that I felt would save my life.

You may know people who say they are "fighting" their cancer. I take nothing from them and their valid and valiant efforts to overcome the dreaded disease. But, as I have said, for me, instead of directly "fighting" and "blocking the blow" each time, I have chosen to invite the power of cancer and bring its force into a place where I felt I could gain some control and redirect the energy to positive purposes.

At the Office

Having survived my cancer experiences partly by using my mental My Chi, I found I could apply it to many other challenging experiences. Here is an example of broadening my use of My Chi into my business life. This example shows how My Chi can be used as a strategic method rather than just an effective conversational tactic or mental self-talk exercise to maintain and power forward through a life-threatening disease.

About ten years into my career, I remember trying to decide how to make a very big decision—to move from one financial services firm to another. I did not feel my current firm was providing either my clients or me with the right products or the right platform of services from which to offer those products. There were better firms, and I felt it was time to move on. However, moving can be fraught with large career risks, the most devastating being that my clients might decide against moving with me.

One of my nicest, biggest, and best clients was also an excellent businessman. I didn't want to lose his business for obvious reasons. The potential punch was if I moved and then he were to tell me he was not going to follow me to the new firm. Applying my mental t'ai chi method from cancer to My Chi people management, I found the power to achieve my objective of keeping him onboard. I decided to invite him into the decision-making process, to engage him and create the dialogue through which I could explain my point of view. Note here how outcomes from My Chi need not be used only in a zero-sum game relationship where one wins and one loses. It is important to once again emphasize that to yield does not mean to surrender in the classic sense, but rather to retreat to a superior position to eventually achieve an objective that can serve all involved.

Rather than set up the move and then tell my key client, I chose to grab the risk his decision posed in advance. I used My Chi preemptively here. If I could get a validation from him that my move was a good one, I then could use his energy to control the situation. To do this, I chose to call him, to engage his excellent business sense and ask him his opinion of my move before moving. I surrendered by bringing him into the decision process. If I achieved his positive response, I had resolved a difficult challenge and further validated the reasons for my move. Alternatively, if he convinced me I shouldn't move, this too would be a good thing actually in my best interest.

I picked up the phone and engaged him in my best version of beginning a My Chi conversation. It went something like this:

> Client picks up. "Hello, Dave."
> Me: "Hi, Bill. Have you a moment to speak?"
> Client: "Sure, what's up?"
> Me: "Bill, It's not about stocks and bonds today. I am facing a business decision, and I respect your wisdom when it comes to these kinds of things. May I run something by you?"
> Client: "Sure. Thanks for thinking of me. Let's see if I can assist."

Me: "To be frank, I am finding that I think I have a better way to serve you and my other clients as well, and I'd really appreciate your perspective. May I lay out some facts for you?"

As you can see, he was flattered I had called him for advice. As the conversation continued, he became intrigued with my thoughts and my reasons for moving. I was perfectly truthful with him and happy I could lay out solid reasons for my move. I focused my reasons clearly on products important to his needs. I described improved services that would improve my service to him directly. I really did appreciate his feedback, new input, and advice. At the end of the call, I heard him say to me, "Dave, I think you are making a good decision here. Just make sure you really focus on the transfer of securities so there are no glitches."

"I'll be darned," I said out loud after I got off the phone. "What a nice guy." Using My Chi had created a win for both of us.

By preemptively reaching out and managing his potential threat by having a dialogue that left us in agreement, no punch was ever thrown. I had drawn him into my situation and ended up in control by using his power to move us both to what turned out to be a better place, pun intended. Importantly, this regards the energy of a person integrally involved in the well-being of my business and his, too. We were not fighting but recognizing similar concepts involved. I had used mental and social My Chi to control a threatening situation. A few weeks later, I moved, and he and virtually all my clients moved as well. In case you're wondering, I am happy to say it turned out to be a wise move for all involved.

My Chi and My Doctors

While I learned to use My Chi in other areas of my life, I can tell you that my best use of the social version was when I used it while negotiating and doing strategic thinking during the search for my surgeons in 2010 after I had been told I had my fourth major recurrence of cancer.

As you know now, I was viewed in a matter-of-fact fashion as inoperable by the first several doctors and cancer centers that Olivia and I visited. The negative opinion of those doctors that no surgical solution was possible constituted the punch I needed to avoid from those doctors. I could not blame them, as they were evaluating their skills and their batting averages as well as my serious case. But my fear was building and really challenging my patience (an opposite of fear) and self-talk efforts. I couldn't afford to believe them. It was by surrendering to a stronger place and not giving in to their opinions that Olivia and I persevered and eventually attracted the team of doctors through my new oncologist. They agreed to do the complicated surgery to which others had said, "Impossible." Let me explain.

Rather than argue or fight with those first few doctors, we did not even engage them beyond a first meeting. They felt they were not capable of working with me. Why try to convince those who consider themselves unqualified or who were advocating some untested approach? Instead, we started doing the most we could at the time. Though it was not what I wanted, it was exactly what the surgeon at M. D. Anderson told us to do as the next best thing: chemotherapy while trying to find the surgeon who would take me on.

I started chemo to try to shrink the tumor enough so that someone might be able to operate in four months. We felt we were embracing what we could do but without giving up on the search for a doctor who would perform an operation to remove my cancerous tumor, as had been done three times before. We realized the two were not mutually exclusive. We could make both efforts. Our embracing my cancer while not settling for half measures was eventually rewarded. The local oncologist who administered the chemo found a team able and willing to do what the medical field calls "heroic" surgery. Doctors say I have been cancer-free for almost five years. I say I may still own it, but I remain true to my motto: I will die with it, not from it.

Shakespeare may have been an early proponent of My Chi. He once wrote: "Your gentleness shall force more than your force moves us to gentleness." Today, we might say, "Kill 'em with kindness." These moments I refer to in dealing with my cancer and the medical community as well the business moments are just a few of the times I used Shakespeare's "gentleness" through My Chi, to advance my cause with minimal disruption in my life and others' lives.

CHAPTER 6

MY CHI AND MY FAMILY

To be able to look back upon one's life in satisfaction is
to live twice.

—Kahil Gibran

The longer I live, the more beautiful life becomes.
—Frank Lloyd Wright

My first mom saw my tendency toward My Chi. Obviously, she didn't call
it t'ai chi or My Chi. She just viewed her son as being polite and, at a young
age, able to think in the moment or on his feet. Somehow, a childlike
attempt at diplomacy (early mental My Chi?) stoked that fire when I was
seven years old in 1952. I realize that was a long time ago in a very different
age, but the gist of the story is timeless.

In the early 1950s, we were just beginning to enjoy what I think of
as the golden age of cars. We were recovered from World War II, and
the technological benefits of American creativity during the war were
washing over the entire domestic economy. Cars were becoming something
everybody could have, and my family was barely able to finally buy a used
1949 Ford four-door sedan. My father and all of us were very proud of
that car.

This was the era of the "Sunday drive" and the origin of the term
Sunday driver. My family and many others used to come home from
church, watch *The Lone Ranger*, and have a bite of lunch. Before getting

to the afternoon chores, we would hop in the car and go nowhere in particular, just any place where it was fun to look through the big windows and enjoy the thrill of the ride. Since we did not have a destination and speed was not an important feature of the trip, we Sunday drivers were the bane of those who were actually in a hurry to get to their destination at a specific time. We usually had great fun on these excursions. It was something we all looked forward to.

On just such a Sunday afternoon, however, the fun in our family car began to fade. We had driven out to a country road, my favorite place on these drives. It was called String Bean Road by our family because it had about a mile of small, short ups and downs, not even really hills. As the car reached the top and went over to the downside of each bean, our stomachs would flip from the momentary weightlessness. I think even though my brother and sister had tired of the experience, the whole family liked to see my huge smiles and uproarious squeals of delight as we went over every crest. We had just finished this part of the trip, and it was time to head home.

I was now quiet, sitting in the middle of the backseat between my thirteen-year-old brother, Bobby, and my nineteen-year-old sister, Peggy, when the whole family, Mom, Dad, older brother, and sister, erupted in a squabble. It started when my sister, who was home on a break from college, announced in what was typical of her strident style then that she was going to spend the rest of the afternoon with former high school friends who were also home from college. My mom and dad had other ideas, such as cleaning up her room, doing the laundry she had brought home, and helping her mother prepare a special family dinner that night.

It became more intense when my brother, never to be outdone by Peggy, chimed in that he wanted to go meet his friends, who were all going to be skating at a pond behind the Sawin family's house until dinner. Talk about throwing another log on the fire! This went on for a while and then really took off, until my dad boomed, "Absolutely not!" to both of them because of their behavior in the car.

Now all four were talking at once as the sound in the car rose in a crescendo. That is, until my dad threatened to stop the car to regain order. If that happened, I knew it would not be good, as my sometimes stubborn dad would not back down from his threat that no one would go anywhere if he actually had to stop the car to calm things. Everyone would remain angry around home for the rest of the day, and I would have no fun at all with any of them.

Things kept going until my dad sent out a warning shot. He touched the brake, and everyone went silent. Everybody seemed to be holding his or her breath as we waited to see what would happen next. Fearless from lack of experience and wanting this to end before the dreaded *stop* occurred, I blurted out in my little boy voice, "Peggy, couldn't you put your laundry in and go see your friends until you think the wash is finished? And Bobby, can you stay home and rake leaves with Dad and me until Peggy gets back to hang laundry and help Mom with dinner? Then, like you said, you can go skating till dinner?"

Everyone looked at everyone else to see what the reaction was. This was a pacifying solution that immediately seemed to please everybody. Everything got done, and somebody was always helping somebody else all afternoon. All seemed stunned, even me—and we didn't *stop*. Whew.

Right then, my mom turned in her front seat, looked back directly into my eyes with a smile I will never forget, and said, "The little diplomat." Well, yeah, I guess so. By reinforcing that moment, she set me on a course. That was a proud moment for this little Dave. That positive comment from my mother was unforgettable. And we happily ended up singing "Ninety-Nine Bottles of Beer on the Wall" all the way home.

Writer David Brooks, in a March 20, 2014 *New York Times* piece, entitled *Going Home Again*, said, "Historical consciousness has a fullness of paradox that future imagination cannot match. When we think of the past, we think about the things that seemed bad at the time but turned out to be good in the long run. We think about the little things that seemed inconsequential in the moment but made all the difference." How true that is for me as I think back to that afternoon.

Now, sixty-some years later, I can see there were the seeds of My Chi in that moment. I wanted everybody to have a fun afternoon and not have everybody, including me, fighting and then moping around the house.

The argument threatened to take the fun away from me. So, out of self-interest, I stepped aside and threw them all off balance. Rather than crying at the upset (fear) or joining the fight by directly shouting at them to stop arguing ("blocking the punch"), my little mind's eye could see only one thing to do, and that was to come up with a solution. Act, rather than react.

Lord knows how it came to me or how I blurted all that out at the time, but as I view it now, my action moved me to a superior position, and I got what I wanted (and so did they) by not joining them in the fight, but by softness and resolution. Because My Chi has been a pattern in my life, it is a fact that I have played the role of pacifier in many relationships.

That is one of the outcomes of using mental My Chi. While disruption creates the moment for My Chi, things usually end peacefully. That afternoon and the fact that I remember it clearly must have been formative as I reminisce and overlay the template of My Chi. As you know, I lost that dear mom when I was eleven, but I can still clearly picture the gentle smile on her face as she looked back over the front seat and said those words.

I will continue to point out My Chi moments in my life. I have learned to respond to my cancer and other events I cite in many of the following chapters using My Chi. Now you have an idea of the derivation of my future descriptions. As I look back in time, these and future moments have My Chi in common.

As I indicated in quoting Brooks's column above, this was not evident to me at the time. It became clear to me about ten years ago. Brooks continues his thought as follows: "Going back is a creative process. The events of childhood are like the Hebrew alphabet; the vowels are missing, and the older self has to make sense of them. Robert Frost's famous poem about the two paths diverging in the woods isn't only about the two paths. It also describes how older people go back in memory and impose narrative order on choices that didn't seem so clear at the time." Doesn't that match up beautifully with Pope's essay? "Whatever is, is right." "All partial evil, universal good." Only with patience can we see the order of things.

Brooks continues his observations: "The person going back home has to invent a coherent tradition out of discrete moments and tease out future implications. He has to see the world with two sets of eyes: the eyes of his own childhood self and the eyes of his current adult self. He has to circle back deeper inside and see parts of himself that were more exposed then than now. No wonder the process of going home again can be so catalyzing." Things inconsequential or very uncomfortable at the time now make sense, seem so formative. "Whatever is, is right."

Casey, my eventual stepmother, was an excellent, unknowing user of this art of My Chi. I now see she used it to manage me and, for a while, my father, to achieve desirable results for all of us. My original sensitivity in the car seems to be the precursor to what became My Chi.

As far as I can figure, she is probably the person I was most in constant contact with as I solidified these valuable problem-solving elements of My Chi. I was blessed by her intuitive use of them in dealing with me and our life situations as parent and stepson. In effect, we egged each other on.

Always Learning

From that time, we fast forward to just a little while ago when I was playing with my little granddaughter, Lucy, while visiting my daughter and family at their home. This event was proof to me that we are always learning; leave it to a child to remind us we are not perfect and to teach us humility and the best life lessons, if we will accept them. Thus, the story that follows of my non-My Chi, blocking response to her literal "punch," and for me, the painful resolution.

If I needed a reminder I am not perfect, this was it. It was like history repeating itself as I recall the self-talk and reset story I related in a previous chapter involving my daughter, Jenny. During a visit to Jenny's home, I was reading the newspaper. Lucy, my capricious, then three-and-a-half-year-old granddaughter, started playfully, lightly hitting my arm. I smiled and ignored the first two or three. This was not unlike my Jenny spilling the nuts, using negative action to attract attention.

When she hit me again, I asked Lucy to stop with a low, firm voice. "Okay, Lucy, it's time to stop." She laughed and tauntingly hit me a little harder, this time not on my arm but on my stomach. I wanted to finish the article I was reading. I knew she was testing me, and at this point, if I had used My Chi, I would have patiently dropped the paper, redirected her, and distracted her with a toy or by turning on the TV. I could have "surrendered" and thereby taken control of the situation by cueing up her favorite movie at the time, *Frozen*. We would have had a nice next hour—and I would have finished the article.

But I didn't have my wits about me. I regret to say I reacted instinctively and with a bit of irritation, which is never good. I literally blocked Lucy's next hit by reflexively raising my hand and grabbing and stopping her wrist in midair as she swung at me. She either grazed my lip with one of her long little fingernails or maybe I bit my lower lip with the surprise at her swing, combined with a flash of anger I should have stifled. I didn't know it then, but a little drop of blood had appeared on my dry lower lip.

Lucy was very surprised at my direct response of grabbing her wrist, and it scared her a little. But she also knew she "had" me by engaging me with her negative action. She quickly became a ball on the floor and began a manufactured version of crying until her dad came in and asked what had happened. She then coyly put me on report. Of course, I felt terrible. I had scared my little granddaughter, and I had embarrassed myself in front of my daughter and son-in-law. *Good grief, I'm a child beater.*

I am happy to say my son-in-law handled things beautifully, including telling me I had a drop of blood on my lip. Yikes. And my dear daughter, while a bit cross with me, forgave me quickly. Even as the incident will forever be etched in my mind, by day's end, Lucy had completely discarded it. The evening ended up with my being on Lucy's bed reading her two bedtime stories. As I think back, how much better it would have been, especially for Lucy and me, if I had used my usual My Chi approach. You can bet I'll never make that mistake with Lucy again.

While I have told of my broadened uses of My Chi, I view it as most valuable in concert with my self-talk and reset approach. This is most true when managing the many facets my cancer. Whether it was informally negotiating with family members or doctors or hospital administrators, there were times when I felt I won the day by using this My Chi thinking to achieve the best for both the other party and me.

I hope this introduction to the concept allows My Chi to begin serving you as well as it has me. It is a pattern that encourages presence of mind, some patience, and thinking on your feet within a pattern, or as a friend said when we were talking about this, "in the moment." I believe anyone can learn to execute this form of patient interaction in critical times. Nobody is perfect, as I proved in my story about Lucy's punch. And believe me, I still miss plenty of putts. But we can always do it right the next time. I find My Chi worth trying to employ every time I sense a challenge, such as my returning cancer or a difficulty in dealing with other people in my life.

CHAPTER 7

RELIGION IS NOT REQUIRED IN HEALING YOURSELF. FAITH IS.

Going to church doesn't make you a Christian any more than standing in a garage makes you a car.

—C. K. Chesterton

Faith Enables Determination

During my four months of chemotherapy treatment in 2010, I had a conversation with a neighbor friend as we walked up the middle of a fairway on our local golf course. I couldn't play at that point, but I could be with my friends anyway. I had learned when it came to cancer, I had to leave it home. I needed to go out and have fun talking about other things and with other people. I focused my self-talk outward with purpose, because my natural tendency seemed to be to focus in to get well.

I had previously shared most all of my "adventures with cancer," including the daunting fourth recurrence, with my friends in the neighborhood, because I knew if I was open about it, my friends would feel more comfortable around me. They wouldn't be worrying that they might make some faux pas. They wouldn't be worrying about what to say, even to the point of avoiding me. So on that day, my dear friend Gene felt comfortable to ask, "Dave, hope you don't mind my asking, but why is it that you don't seem discouraged at all?"

Part of my golf gang – Bob, Gene, me, Mike and Dave

I answered as simply as I could what I thought of as a very tough but real question from a good friend. "Gene, I experience those times, but only briefly when I'm alone or only with Olivia. However, regardless of the situation, I've learned to reset myself with my self-talk quickly, especially when I'm with you guys. What good would it do any of us if I allowed myself to be grumpy and fearful? I think the reasons I stay 'up' come down to two key words: *faith* and *determination*. And really, I think faith enables determination to do important things we want to or believe we have to do."

For me, faith instills commitment to my goals and resolutions. Faith keeps me going long after I have met with moments of discouragement. Gene didn't realize it, but he had asked me about my number-one goal, which is to die with this cancer, not from it.

Faith is like the flying buttresses of a Gothic cathedral. It strengthens and supports the structure.

As a former navy guy, to me, faith is like the interior ribs built into the understructure of a ship that reinforce the outer hull. In rough seas, it is that understructure that holds the ship together and on course to complete the journey. Without that understructure of ribs, the hull would collapse when tested in rough seas. I have seen and talked with fellow cancer patients who are short on those underlying ribs of faith. Their struggles have seemed so much bigger to them, and even to me, as we have talked.

Determination based on faith is a powerful force that—to continue the seagoing analogy—has provided me with the courage and emotional strength to cut through those battering waves of cancer. Rationally, there were times when there were no data points indicating I was going to survive my last run-in in 2010. At those times, faith-filled self-talk and looking for the good to come was all that kept me plowing forward into the waves of challenges that just kept coming, especially during chemotherapy.

Importantly, as I have explained, determination is different from, and does not require, fighting cancer to overcome the disease. Fighting implies denial by definition, and I have never denied my cancer. I have tried to accept and embrace my cancer.

"Obstacles are those frightful things you see when you take your eyes off your goals," said Henry Ford.

We all have goals, even if we have not clearly identified them. For me, clarifying them by occasionally writing them down was certainly a valuable exercise that further empowered me to use faith-infused determination to succeed at reaching my goals. To write, I have to think about the subject. I have to think about what I am trying to achieve, to form the words in my mind and express them. This is a more structured version of self-talk. This alone created some clarity for me. At a minimum, I could see I had to set and achieve numerous short-term goals to achieve the final goal of being well again. This is not unlike making a shopping list, when the bigger goal is to be ready for a dinner party over the weekend.

My wife and I—mostly my wife, bless her heart—had to make the calls to medical facilities, find surgeons who might be qualified, and, even tougher, willing to perform my operation. We had to set up the appointments and travel arrangements to have the critical conversations that would eventually mean life or death for me. Was it worth it to go through this tedious process to reach each and especially our ultimate goal? You bet it was. I'm still here. Keep on keepin' on.

Determination keeps us going, but faith gives us the courage to initiate. Faith enables determination. It gives us courage and brings into focus what we need to do. Remember the saying, "a pint of courage," referring to the fact that some people, even I, have been known to take a drink when scared? Drinking and/or taking drugs beyond medical prescription is not a courageous act. It merely masks the problem for a while. It is an attempt to run away (flight) from the challenge or problem rather than confront it, deal with it, and end it. Nelson Mandela said, "Courage is not the absence of fear, but the triumph over it." Drinking does not end the problem; it is there the next morning. Faith is courage without the bottle. Martin Luther King once said, "Faith is taking the first step even though you don't see the whole staircase." He believed it is our responsibility to act. I believe faith is a powerful enabler.

A Focused Lens

Faith is a lens through which I can see everything more clearly. It keeps my self-talk grounded when creeping fear begins to create disillusionment and disappointment. I reset more quickly when I reference my thoughts through my faith.

Faith helps me keep my thoughts and self-talk in focus—in context with the bigger picture surrounding the challenge that has my immediate attention. Think about my friend and my verbal exchange above: It was a conversation about my huge challenge to survive my fourth onslaught of cancer. I felt like I had a double-barreled shotgun at my head. I hadn't yet found a surgeon who would agree to operate on me, and I was suffering the punishing effects of chemo as we talked.

Things seemed to be going backward. Yet my faith allowed me to keep my perspective. As such, I wasn't going to let my cancer rob me of being with my friends. Despite cancer's ability to make us turn inward and feel like we want to just stay home and try to feel better, I wasn't about to give up doing what we had all really enjoyed doing together for years.

Leave It Home

The insidious disease drives us toward feeling alone and avoiding outside contact. This is true for the patient and can be true for the caregiver as well. There is an unexpected quality here. My intuitive reaction was to pull back from life. This felt especially true when the chemo effects started to rob me of my physical self through hair loss, weight loss, and loss of strength. But leave it home. I self-talked to myself (and so did Olivia) to go out and have fun talking about other things and being with people. Faith helped me focus outward with purpose and ignore my natural tendency to focus in, either to feel sorry for myself or to concentrate on getting well. Neither was the best choice, even though that seemed the natural reaction.

My Version of Faith

Now please understand. I am not trying to preach or define other persons' versions of faith. I am trying to give you, dear reader, context in which you may better understand how my faith and my self-talk enable me. I have been asked by people, upon hearing my story, "Well, Dave, what do you have faith in? What do you believe in?" It is my experience that everyone has his own version of and definition of faith. I know I have mine. Here are a couple of thoughts.

First of all, my faith is not exclusionary; it is inclusionary. I welcome diverse beliefs by others. A friend of mine once said, "The most expensive thing a man can own is a closed mind."

It seems to me it is important to believe in something. For me, it is God. I also try my best to adhere to Judeo-Christian values as a way of living my life. For me, the life of Christ stands full of examples of how I can best meet life's challenges through the years. And for a perfect example of Alexander Pope's "all partial evil, universal good," look at the end of Christ's life. From the partial evil of disciple Judas's betrayal of Christ to the Romans and Christ's persecution and death on the cross comes the truly universal good of his resurrection and promise of eternal life for his followers. Whether you believe the story of Christ or not, reading and understanding the principles of and point of the story of his life are wonderful reminders of what faith can be and do for us.

For others, it may be believing in gods or adhering to a set of principles, such as those we see in Buddhism, or just believing there is a less-defined higher being or force. In my mind, even *not* believing is still having a belief system. Simplistically, an agnostic believes in nothing because he cannot confirm the existence of a god. An atheist claims to be irreligious.

These two views seem analogous to the color black on a color wheel. Some define black as the absence of color, but in my mind, black is still a color. An agnostic's or even an atheist's version of faith could be just that he has faith in himself or humanity, but I believe that it is still a worthwhile, even imperative effort to try to clearly define a belief system: your personal faith. Otherwise, by being faithless, we become cynical. We will talk about cynicism a little later.

Decide. Choose. Defining and refining your faith will equip you with a critical and constant point of reference. It will probably evolve as you grow older and experience and expose your mind to other people's ways of thinking, just as mine has. But as Charles Murray says in his book *The Curmudgeon's Guide to Getting Ahead*, take religion seriously. Whatever your version of it is, it will give you a grounding, or as I said, a lens through which to see everything in life more clearly. When I get up in the morning, I say a quick prayer of thanks. I joke with people that I am just thankful to see the ceiling another morning. With what I've been through, it means I'm still around. But it's more than that. By giving thanks, I am centering myself for the day. I am focusing on how many blessings I have and starting my day with that positive outlook.

While the specifics of my belief system may be of no consequence to you, on the chance they will spur your thinking, here are a couple of other key pieces. Also, I feel I owe this glimpse to you, the reader, so you know my point of reference through the rest of the book.

As I said, I believe in one God. While I grew up going to church with my family almost every Sunday in a Protestant setting, over the years, I have ranged around to several Protestant denominations including Dutch Reformed, Episcopal, Unitarian, and Presbyterian. Religion, as opposed to faith, in my experience, can be divisive. As a child and then as a married adult with young children, I felt obligated to and enjoyed attending a specific church consistently, and I benefited from that experience in meaningful ways, I am sure. But now, while I have not attended the same denominated church consistently for decades, I have and still do experience frequent periods of true reverence every week. I express my faith through prayers daily, often informally. In fact, I view praying as an offshoot of my self-talk.

I believe everyone has some good in him or her, including a killer in prison. You have heard the saying, "Only his mother could love him." She sees the good we don't. But we don't have to be naive to let our self-talk focus on the good. No matter how much or how little good we think is in the situation or the person involved, it gives me a positive mindset with which to proceed without being blind to part of the situation or the person. Focusing on the good allows me to be a skeptic, not a cynic.

Besides the question my friend Gene asked, people have also asked me, "Dave, why didn't you say, 'Why me?'" the first time and each successive time I found out I had cancer. I really find it hard to answer this question without crediting the existence of my faith. Instead, my question was, "Okay, what do I do now?" Rather than looking backward, I wanted to look forward and act quickly in the present to find the good as soon as possible. I wanted to move forward to solve, not look back and complain or fear the future. Conquer, don't complain.

From a slightly different angle on this subject, while I wanted to move forward and out of the disease, there are some who, while not complaining, take their time getting well. I know a lady who had open-heart surgery and survived in good shape. After recuperation, she just couldn't help wearing the sort of blouse to work every day, warm or cold, rain or shine, that highlighted her breastbone scar, front and center. For a long time, it was her badge, her potential conversation piece. Hey, she made it! Good for her. This I see as different from the debilitating, complaining syndrome. In fact, I'm kind of proud of her, too.

I also have seen several sick people, whether from cancer or some other serious disease, enjoy the attention, the almost celebrity status suddenly lavished on them by friends, family, and acquaintances. The psychology is understandable and similar to that of the open-heart surgery survivor. Maybe it is not terribly attractive, but as long as it doesn't blossom into complaining, I see it as harmless.

However, if such an approach tempts the person to prolong the process of being sick and then the recovery time as well, there are subtle dangers, not the least of which is infection from visits to medical centers. The celebrity attitude has diminishing returns and can be unwise, but I still see it as markedly different from complaining and whining, "Woe is me."

People who have these reactions to their disease are not driven by a lack of faith, but by vanity—or inner loneliness.

I have lost friends to cancer. I have been asked by their relatives, "Why did he die?" And maybe it was just me, but I have thought they might also be asking without saying, "And why are you still alive?" This challenges their faith and mine. I met a very nice lady at dinner on a recent trip to visit friends. Her husband had died suddenly about six months earlier. Life had been fine until one day, when he was doing small projects in the backyard, a swarm of bees broke free from a beekeeper's hive next door and streamed over the fence. Bees like water, and he was cleaning the pool nearby. They headed toward the pool, startled him, and his reactive movement apparently threatened them. The bees stung him again and again. He was pronounced brain dead at the hospital and taken off life support. My friends who had introduced me to her later told me she could not reconcile her husband's death and became very depressed. For months, she had been fighting feelings of depression and had even had thoughts of suicide.

As my friends and I talked, I finally said, "You know what? We humans just have to get used to the idea we don't know everything. Remember, our kind used to think the world was flat. We still can't reconcile major issues." I admit I became a bit agitated and continued my thought, saying,

> "Tell you what, next time you see her, ask her where the end of outer space is. What comes next? According to our understanding, we can't define The End because we humans have a set of concepts that don't reconcile. After our universe, there is always something 'next' and next after that. What is The End? If she can answer that, maybe we can answer why her husband died—and why I didn't. I only hope she will consider what her husband would want for her. I'm sure it would be the return of her happiness, rather than her contemplating suicide."

That sounds quite callous, but the fact that we don't have the answer to many "big" questions must mean we have a number of assumptions wrong, even in this twenty-first century. It is a hard thought to accept when we feel so "modern" with our constant technological advances. But have patience. At some point, we just have to rely on our faith that there is a grand plan that includes our destiny. Only then can we achieve some peace. Those sad moments we experience at times in the short span of our lives must be met head-on. We must use our faith to reassure ourselves all will be right in the long run. This is the essence of Pope's "An Essay on Man," made clear when he states, "Whatever is, is right."

So our faith enables peace of mind and self-determination within the frame of our destiny. That combination should make us incredibly effective. But unfortunately, many people—including me, at times—can still be self-limiting. Those with gray hair may remember cartoon character Pogo, who said, "We have met the enemy and he is us!" This can be so true.

Faith, Self-Limitation, and Doctors

I can get caught up in the idea that a doctor knows all; therefore, I won't challenge him or her. This is not the doctor's fault. I blindly begin to believe the doc is a final arbiter. I'm a skeptic, but once I have selected a doctor, I have faith in him or her. I am able to commit to finding the best course of action with him. I have tried to train my self-talk to gather courage and continue asking questions even though I may not like the reply. I try to do so in a friendly way, because I want to be informed for my own benefit, not tick off the doctor with my attitude. I have always tried to partner up with my doctors and stay informed and involved.

An insidious self-limiter for me has been, believe it or not, my positive attitude. The doctor may say, "What's wrong, Dave? What is bothering you?" And I answer, "Oh, nothing, Doc. I'm doing okay." When I haven't broken through these self-limiting moments, Olivia, as my dear wife and caregiver, has jumped in with a little exasperation, but a lot of goodwill, and made statements and asked the questions out loud that I had asked myself and her when we were alone together at home.

She knew there were times I just couldn't seem to vocalize my questions when looking at the doctor in his office. In my younger days, we were taught not to complain about injuries and physical ailments. I still can't quite break away from that, even when it isn't really complaining. I have cancer, for goodness sake! Also, while I was the guy who was sick, maybe I just didn't want to admit how sick I was or hear the answer. That's a version of denial I couldn't help using sometimes.

There's no doubt that being in a doctor's office can be an intimidating experience. Finding a way to overcome that feeling is an important step in the process of getting well. My self-talk kept telling me, "Don't be self-limiting."

That said, there were some doctors who we both felt were not going to work for us; we had the wrong chemistry, or they had ideas that just did not make sense, given what we knew already and had studied. We were right to doubt them as we did. We felt the right answer was still out there somewhere, and with persistence and faith, we continued to seek it.

I think part of the reason I am here today sitting at this table writing is because I found my way to:

- Exercise constantly my faith to help me keep my positive perspective while meeting my challenges.
- Ask and keep asking tough questions of my health professionals (or let my wife do so). Doing so, I largely avoided being self-limiting.
- Be a skeptic willing to challenge by asking questions, but then able to completely accept what we believed was valid information and completely believe in the people/doctors who were involved. I never became a cynic, always looking for the gloom and saying, "Why me?"

Whether you reach a state of happiness in life has little to do with your circumstances; it has much more to do with your attitude, your faithful courage, your determination and your choices.

My faith enabled my determination to always choose to find a way to "keep on keepin' on" and, in time, overcome some pretty steep odds. Richard Carlson, PhD, wrote a book in the late 1990s called *Don't Sweat the Small Stuff... and It's All Small Stuff*. After four pretty big challenges from being diagnosed with cancer, I couldn't agree with him more. There's very little that can make me unhappy for long. I just reset, and soon, there's a smile on my face.

As an end to this chapter, here are some thoughts I carry forward with me that you might like to contemplate.

> Life can only be understood backwards, but it must be lived forwards.
>
> —Soren Kierkegaard

> Impatience is dangerous to your faith.
>
> —David A. Bantz

Riddle me this—I'm lucky: I've had cancer for 28 years.

My version of faith does not necessarily require the restrictive, self-regulating good boy or girl that most religions do. The faith I am referring to has very little to do with whether you sleep with someone, take a drink, or are gluttonous. However, by saying this, I do not deny the value of those time-tested Judeo-Christian moral rules. They do a pretty good job of being the guardrails in our lives. To wit, Blaise Pascal was a French philosopher who lived in the 1600s. He devised Pascal's Wager, which posits that all humans must bet their lives either that God exists or he doesn't. Given there is a possibility that God does exist, there is the possibility of infinite gain (eternity in heaven). So a rational person would choose to believe in God or at least live as though he does exist. If he does not exist, the person would have only finite losses of some pleasures, luxuries, and other acts considered sins worthy of damning the person to hell. Guess we should play it safe.

Finally, faith encourages us to use our self-talk in a powerful way to shape our efforts to create goodness in our lives—including health, in my case—and to enable achievement and happiness for ourselves and others.

CHAPTER 8

BREAKING AWAY

One meets his destiny often on the road he takes to avoid it.
—French proverb

After my mother's death, when my dad was home, he spent months mourning, moping around the house. I was just eleven, but I remember very well one night during our first year without her, when I asked him a question about Mother. He teared up, told me not to ask about her ever again, and then fell into the couch and cried and cried. I cried, too. I felt so bad—worse about hurting him that moment than about my mom. So our conversations from then on were no deeper than those of daily life. I didn't ever say another word about her. I can tell you it hurts to this day, because my memories of her dimmed so much without the repetition of stories that go with revering someone you love after her death.

Dad and me

Dad at an evening fund-raiser with guests Ronald and Nancy Reagan

Any and all self-talk I was doing became negative and discouraging. Was I to blame somehow? For a while after my mother's death, my dad didn't know what was going on with me or how I felt inside. Those years left scars beyond those from losing my mom. I was still a good kid inside, so I survived and, unbeknownst to me at the time, was toughened by those troubled times in ways that were to come in to play when I began my twenty-five-year-plus journey with cancer.

Decades after high school—five, to be exact—I was attending our fiftieth high school reunion and one of my neighborhood friends, Jimmy Beggs, remembered with a wry smile that a lot of windows, lights, and other things were damaged during those years after my mom died. Juvenile delinquency could easily have grown into something nasty for me. My dad was often tied up late in the day at his office. It seemed he was always busy with board meetings and evening fundraising affairs because he was a YMCA executive. He not only ran the local YMCA and associated camps; he also had to raise the money from the community to keep the branch and camps operating. This meant lots of appearances and dinners kept him out late.

So back then, much as he didn't want it to happen, I was alone many nights until 8:00 p.m. or later. One day, when I got home from school, there was a lady in the house, cleaning. My dad had hired this lady, Mrs. Cranston, to clean, and while doing so, she was supposed to keep an eye on me. Which was her priority, I wondered? Apparently, Dad had heard about one or two (or more!) issues in the neighborhood, and he realized I needed some supervision when I came home from school. Cleaning was secondary. I did not like her being there, and she didn't really want to fulfill my dad's hopes of her being my supervisor, so she wasn't thrilled with my presence either.

I think my dad was very lenient with me during this time because he felt bad for me. One Fourth of July, he actually gave me a big bag of firecrackers. My curiosity was piqued one day after I got home from school and didn't have anything to do other than homework, and that was out of the question until my dad got home and made me do it. I asked myself, "Does a firecracker, specifically a bright-red cherry bomb, go off under water? And where is some water close by I can use for an experiment?" Of course. You guessed it; the upstairs toilet was perfect.

69

So I lit the cherry bomb and dropped it in the toilet and ran out of there. *Kablaam! Clunk! Swissshh.* Well, I was okay with the *kablaam,* but not the *clunk* and *swish.* I opened the door and there, on the floor, was approximately half of the toilet bowl in one piece—*clunk.* The other half was still standing in place. The water had quickly left the standing half and was now around my shoes and on the rest of the floor—*swish.* Uh-oh. That was bad. As Mrs. Cranston came running up the stairs, I grabbed a hammer leaning against the wall in the hall that my dad had been using to repair damage to a baseboard.

She said, "Are you okay?" and then screamed, "What happened?" I said I had been going to the bathroom and dropped the hammer and it had hit the toilet just the wrong way. Really, I did tell her that. Of course, she didn't believe me (even I didn't believe me), but I think she was unable to shake the mental picture of a male standing at the toilet flipping a hammer while going to the bathroom. She stuttered and could not debate me about it—and called my dad at work.

Now I really didn't like her. He was upset, but my dad chose to believe me later on that night. What a guy. He truly loved me, probably to a fault. By the way, he never could figure out how all the little red dots had appeared all over the bathroom ceiling (from the red dye in the cherry bomb).

About two weeks later, Mrs. Cranston was upstairs when I got home. She had finished dusting and cleaning the whole downstairs, including the living room. I didn't want to go upstairs to my room for multiple reasons, her being up there the biggest. So I resumed my mission with the firecrackers.

There was a big fireplace in the living room, and we had not cleaned it since the fire Dad and I had a few days earlier while having grilled cheese sandwiches on TV trays and watching the Walt Disney program together. I thought that might be a safe place to try another experiment with my firecrackers. I now knew cherry bombs were waterproof and pretty powerful. And I knew I shouldn't try the M-80 silver firecracker I had in my hand in the water for fear of another *clunk, swish.*

So, I dropped the M-80 in the fireplace, and oh … my … gosh, it was loud in the house. I heard Mrs. Cranston flying down the stairs already informing me of her opinion of my latest experiment. But that was nothing compared to when she arrived in the living room and found she was looking at me through a gray haze of ashes in the air. I don't think my dad was very happy with her dusting job when he got home. She didn't even take the time to call my dad. For some reason, she left for the day right after seeing me standing there looking at the haze with a sheepish smile. My mission was succeeding. I think she was getting the idea. But my dad hadn't yet gotten it.

Then came the coup de grace, which at the time I thought was nothing short of genius. As I look back as an adult, I question that evaluation, but I'll let you decide. You see, we recently had been to visit my Grandma in Ohio. In the fourth-floor attic of the turn-of-the-century house in Columbus, I found my grandfather's old nonfunctioning, 1850s vintage, single-barrel shotgun. I loved it, and Dad let me take it home. Now, I still had some firecrackers left; the little two-inch stick-shaped ones that you are probably familiar with even now. I thought it would be marvelous to drop a lit firecracker down the barrel and see if it sounded like a real shot fired from the old gun. I also thought maybe Mrs. Cranston would like to see how I did it.

So I dropped the lit firecracker down the barrel, leveled the gun against my shoulder, and stepped into the dining room where Mrs. Cranston was hard at it polishing some silver. I said, "Mrs. Cranston?" She looked up to see the barrel of the gun front-on. *Blllaaaaammmmm!* And fire spit out of the barrel about a foot long, surprising even me. Who knew?

Mrs. Cranston's final check was probably significantly larger than usual. I got in real trouble and lost my firecracker privileges later that night. Dad finally got it—and Mrs. Cranston was gone.

This sort of behavior, which you and I may find humorous, graduated in frequency and seriousness during the next three years. Other episodes included breaking a huge plate-glass window at a school with a rock (and getting caught), shooting out streetlights, shooting out neighbors' porch lights, and shooting out the window of a passing car with a BB gun (and getting caught).

Cancer had robbed my dad and me of the dearest person in our lives. Now I was squandering my childhood with these reactions to my terrible loss and his resulting remoteness. Cancer has effects that reach far beyond the patient, and my family was experiencing it. I was a bony, anorexic kid during the two years leading up to my mom's death. Maybe I should add that kids are smart, including me at the time. Even back then, when parents used to "hide" the disease, we little ones knew. I can still vividly remember standing outside my mom's bathroom door asking why she was in there so long. My dad, if he was home, would nervously shoo me away when I hung around. I ate so little my dad used to try to incent me by saying I ate like a bird. I imagine the worry about my mom drove my anorexia.

Now between the ages of eleven and thirteen, my constant acts of vandalism were clear indications to my father that we were (meaning I was) headed into more and more trouble. Dad was thoroughly dismayed at my terrible grades and now these troubles. A psychologist might say I was acting out my loss, loneliness, and unhappiness. Maybe, but people kept telling my dad what a great kid I was with so much potential. My dad heard that about me constantly, but the wonderful and caring guy had no clue how to solve the problems he saw developing.

Or so I thought. But things were happening behind the scenes. Certainly, this thirteen-year-old troublemaker had no idea. In the third year after my mom died, what seemed like a miracle began to unfold. All partial evil, universal good. One day, seeming to me out of the blue, Dad brought a wonderful lady home to visit. She was visiting from Charleston, West Virginia. She and my dad had known each other during their years at Ohio State decades ago. Apparently, months earlier, he had developed the courage to call her, and everything had clicked since then.

Six months after her visit, they were engaged, and marriage came soon after that. You can guess I did not perceive her in any way like Mrs. Cranston. My negative self-talk was firmly in control during those days. I was a mess, but I was still hanging on. I just needed a small spark. I look back and think of how gracefully Casey accepted me as her stepson and quietly made me her "project."

For others who have gone through a period like I did and recovered, it may have been through involvement with the wonderful Big Brothers Big Sisters program, the YMCA, Boy Scouts, or some other entity or person who engages troubled youth. For me, it was Casey. She became my partner as much as a parent.

By the way, my final act as a vandal unfortunately involved Casey and was appropriately climactic. I hit a "perfect" nine-iron golf shot from the far corner of our backyard toward the house. Why toward the house, I'll never know, other than risking being destructive once more. It was perfect because it went a long way—and right through a back basement window of our house. The window shattered. Casey was standing below that window about to load the washing machine. She and her laundry basket were showered with glass. I cannot tell you how bad I felt when I heard her scream. Amazingly, she was not hurt. As I picked the shards of glass from the laundry while apologizing profusely to her, I all at once realized how stupid I had been being doing these kinds of things. Suddenly, I wanted to be on my best behavior around her forevermore.

CHAPTER 9

THE NUMBER 28, HOMEWORK, AND HAPPINESS

Happiness is pleasure without regret.

—Leo Tolstoy

In everybody's life, there are moments we can look back on and know they were critical. For me, this scary golf shot was one of them, and somehow, even in my moping state, I realized it. As I said, from my point of view, my new stepmother arrived out of nowhere. I was unprepared for her arrival, but I chose to accept her rather than have her be my next Mrs. Cranston.

I'm not sure why, but I didn't perceive her as competition for my dad's attention. I didn't see her as a substitute for my dad like Mrs. Cranston. I knew I was lonely and unhappy, and I saw a way out with this friendly lady from West Virginia. She was a very kind and happy person. As it turned out, she awakened in me latent ways of thinking that not only bolstered me then, but also became patterns that saved my life during my twenty-five-year journey with my killer disease. One particular way of thinking she awakened in me was understanding the big difference between wanting something and needing something. Then she helped me differentiate pleasure and happiness. Sounds simple, right? Before reading on, take your best shot at explaining the differences.

Wanting versus Needing

Okay, now let's see how close your versions are to mine. First let's see how learning to differentiate wanting from needing impacted my life and might be impacting yours.

Wanting versus needing is the simpler of the two comparatives. In simplest terms, let's use a child's life. A little four-year-old like my granddaughter Lucy wants a toy car to play with. She needs food that will be put in front of her at dinner. (She may also want the food, but she definitely *needs* the food.) When it is dinnertime, the toy car may likely be cast aside as interest for the food grows. If her parents were given a choice of only a toy car or a dinner in the next forty-eight hours, is there any doubt they would choose the food because it is a necessity? The parents know she can do without the toy car, but eventually, she will need the food.

My wife would say of me, I want new golf clubs, but I do not need them.

Pleasure versus Happiness

The difference between experiencing pleasure and happiness is parallel to the difference between wanting and needing. The differences are not just semantic. In each of these cases, one is *not* the other.

Pleasure comes from taking immediate gratification. Pleasure is the equivalent of the child wanting the toy car. But the gratification will not last; it will likely turn into displeasure. We parents know that even though she has the car, she'll be screaming for the needed food soon.

A common example dealing with pleasure is trying to lose weight. Uh-oh. You decide to give in to eating something you want but do not need. You immediately sense pleasure as you eat that piece of dark chocolate cake. Great. However, soon, the short-term pleasure turns into disgust with yourself—and more weight. When you get home from the restaurant, you realize you caused a setback to your goal of losing weight. What started as the positive feeling of pleasure turns into feeling bad about yourself and sets the stage for negative self-talk.

Dr. Elizabeth Dunn, an associate professor of psychology at the University of British Columbia, co-authored a study of fifty-five people she brought in to her lab to sample some chocolate. One group was sent home after the tasting and told not to have any chocolate for a week, with the expectation they would return to have the samples again. Participants in another group got a fancy bag of chocolates and were told to eat as much as they wished during the week before returning. The third and last group was given sample chocolates with no instructions at all and served as the control group for the study.

A week later, the groups returned to sample chocolates in the lab again. Various other studies have shown that repeated experiences over time, regardless of their nature, usually cause a decline in the pleasure people get from those experiences. This was true of all participants who had eaten the chocolates during the week. The people who abstained from the chocolate for the week turned out to be the only ones who enjoyed the chocolate this second tasting as much as the first time. I mention this study because it shows the pleasure factor for those who indulged in the midweek had declined, but the pleasure of those who did not, remained. Was there a conversion of pleasure to happiness from the personal discipline of abstention? This was not a stated conclusion of the study in so many words, but I think that was an X factor that this study revealed.

Happiness is a longer-term experience. It comes from feeling you can exert some control over your life. Just as need is a more permanent real emotion than want, happiness feels real compared to the ephemeral feeling of gratification through pleasure. Having worked hard at dieting and exercising, you are happier being and feeling thinner and knowing that your efforts made a difference with lasting impact. Happiness is a byproduct of effort. It leads to and reinforces positive self-talk and creates peace of mind. You have a feeling of accomplishment.

The Number 28

Soon after my parents returned from their honeymoon, Stepmom Casey went to a parent-teacher conference and found out I had failed to turn in twenty-eight math homework assignments. Let's say my graceful stepmom was not pleased. Thus began part of her quest to bring me out of my lazy, low-self-esteem shell. Before Casey arrived, I took pleasure in going out to play rather than doing my homework. The more I fell behind in those math assignments, the more easily I convinced myself with my self-talk that I was bad at math. "See? Here's the evidence," my self-talk said. "Here's my D+ on this pop quiz."

This pattern created a self-fulfilling view in my mind. I really did become bad at math; that is, I was behind in what I needed to know. Learning math requires what is called building-block learning. In other words, once I blew off the first ten homework assignments, I had sealed my fate, or so I thought.

If you are studying a language and you do not study the vocabulary first, you will not be able to advance to forming sentences. So, I could not understand and compute the tougher math problems as the semester went along. Succinctly, I was in trouble—again. I felt no happiness about myself. Short-term gratification from playing rather than studying were my negative forms of pleasure, and they rapidly devolved to my feeling bad about myself. I was ashamed, and my self-talk was really letting me have it.

Maybe my teacher had tried to convey thoughts about staying up-to-date in my homework and explaining building-block, or cumulative, learning to me, but when Casey did, it was different.

Consistently, she chose to lead me, not push me. She was not goading me, scolding me, and shaming me. She may have been furious inside, and it would have been her pleasure to let those feelings out. But she chose to keep her emotions in check and to determine actions and words that would achieve the long-term goal of turning me into the good student she and the teacher knew I could be.

We did not know it then, but as I look back, I see My Chi at work here. Stepping back by keeping her emotions in check, she surrendered to a higher position, even though she was probably very angry with me. She decided against releasing her anger. Instead, Casey gained a stronger position by redirecting the energy from those feelings into an effort to lead and motivate me. She focused on the long-term goal of helping me to grow and find happiness rather than the short-term pleasure she could have experienced by berating me.

She didn't become a friend like some parents try to do (such an effort is an error, in my opinion). Instead, she became more of a partner, just as she did when we tried to help my dad find joy after they married. We explored solutions together. After talks with her, I was uplifted and inspired and drawn in, rather than feeling beaten down and embarrassed. I frankly can't remember exactly what she negotiated with the teacher regarding the twenty-eight assignments. I vaguely remember the teacher chose parts of them that I had to do under her guidance so I could catch up.

No matter. The point is Casey had taken an interest, and she wanted me to succeed. And importantly, I knew it. So she and the teacher partnered up (there's that word *partner* again; remember it for later) to create a path for me to put the building blocks in place quickly. I was able to catch up with the class and not just survive the semester, but actually prepare for my junior and senior years.

I view this time and this event as another one of those major turning points for me. Given the chance, I actively chose to convert my motives and actions with Casey's encouragement. I had been experiencing the momentary pleasure of having playtime by not studying. The cheap thrills from my small-time vandalism and ensuing paranoia the next day in class with no homework to turn in changed into the longer-term happiness of being a prepared, up-to-date student.

At school, other kids and especially teachers had thought of me as the nice little kid whose mom had died and who was always in trouble. I remember back to when the teachers used to say to my dad, "Mr. Bantz, your son has so much potential." Later, my father told me that comment was one of the worst backhanded compliments he could have heard, because it meant I was an underachiever. I was really doing poorly, and I shouldn't have been. But with Casey's involvement and leadership, I changed a lot of minds. I actually became one of the good students. My self-talk had reversed. Teachers saw the improvement and began to expect good performance from me.

Improvement like that gets rewarded, and the teachers really began to take an interest in me. My grades took off, and I felt wonderful. This was different than pleasure; it was happiness. Casey stepped into the background as I began to respond to this wonderful new paradigm at school. I went on to have reasonably good grades in my junior and senior years, good enough to earn acceptance at several colleges, including the University of Vermont and Wake Forest College (now University) in North Carolina. Those were amazing years.

My self-talk—actually, my whole self-image—completely reversed. I look back and think of how I surprised not only the teachers at school, but myself. This big initial jump in positive effort led to positive self-talk, which led to an upward spiral of positive effort and then self-talk, leading to a more positive outcome, leading to more positive self-talk, leading to more positive outcomes; you get it. I couldn't identify it back then as I do now, but I knew I was on a roll. My cheerful self-talk told me so.

Finally, I was a kid experiencing and expressing happiness. I had no time for vandalism anymore. Casey had started the engine, and I was a willing vehicle that drove all of us, especially my father, through three very happy years.

Then suddenly, when I was just sixteen, my father's unexpected and earth-shaking death impacted the summer before my senior year. This was a whole new challenge to my newfound positive self-talk and Alexander Pope-inspired emerging understanding of my faith.

CHAPTER 10

DO IT ANYWAY

The race is not always to the swift, but to those who keep
running.
—Anonymous quote on a small desk sign about
determination that was my daughter Jenny's gift during
my first bout with cancer in 1986

What is success, and how does self-talk affect it? Oh, my. So much has
been written about the topic of success, and very good books are available
in your bookstore, on Amazon, and in your local library. But it is a key
aspect of why we do what we do every day and the self-talk we have every
day, so I'd like to address it here.

Many have tried to whittle the word *success* down to a profound, short
phrase or one-sentence definition. Maybe they have succeeded, maybe
not, but I found my version. I chose my definition while reading a speech
by Albert E. N. Gray, a former president of Prudential Insurance. It was
in a little handbook, "The Common Denominator of Success," which the
company produced many years ago to hand out to its agents. Mr. Gray
made the speech at Prudential headquarters in Dryden Hall, Newark, New
Jersey. It was potent. A friend of Casey's talked with me about starting a
career selling insurance after college and gave it to me. In so doing, he did
me a favor much bigger than he may ever have realized.

I acquired the booklet from him during one of what I call my "lost
sheep" moments in life. Have you had one of those times when everything

should be going great, you're still young, the stars seem aligned, but ... but ... nothing is happening? Every time I think back to that time, it reminds me of the 1967 movie *The Graduate* with Dustin Hoffman and Katherine Ross (a great movie even now, by the way). I was in the same position as Dustin's character, except nobody said "plastics." I have had several of those moments in my life, and this was one of them.

I was a college senior in 1966, during the Vietnam War draft build-up, and I faced the end of my college experience without any job prospects. Truth is, I majored in sociology. For all the wonderful things I have said about my stepmom, she will not go down in the hall of fame as a college curriculum or career advisor. I really didn't have an idea about how to get started looking for job prospects. I had already acquired a key ingredient of success by this time: determination. But I had nowhere to apply it. To paraphrase H. Jackson Browne Jr., I was like an octopus on roller skates. There was lots of effort, but I never knew if it was going to make me go forward, backward, or sideways.

I went home on a semester break to Charleston, West Virginia, and Casey realized I was adrift and challenged. I was a perfect military draft prospect. She went into action creating various meetings with some of her male friends—the "dad factor," she called it—to try to advise me and awaken me to thinking about the draft and careers in general.

We had moved to Charleston during my college years, so that is where I went "home." It was Casey's old home, not mine. I knew very few people there, and those few were all my age. However, Casey had some kind and capable adult friends in the community. Gaston Caperton II, a gentleman in every sense of the word, was one of them. You may recognize the name because his son, Gaston Caperton III, later became governor of West Virginia.

Mr. Caperton, owner of a successful insurance brokerage, gave me the unassuming three-inch by five-inch paperback book and a talk about insurance and being successful in general. His message and the message in the book with the speech were simple and powerful. Basically, the common denominator was: "Successful people do the things that failures don't like to do."

Huh! Isn't that another version of determination? *Could it be that simple?* I asked myself. I realized the short answer was yes. And that started my engines running in a healthy direction for the rest of my life. As I grew during this period, my self-talk was telling me, "Always do a little more than is asked of you," to drive that determination idea home. In a competitive world, lots of people do good things. But that little or marginal extra effort is uncommon. It became a follow-on affirmation in my self-talk and remains with me to this day. I call it an owner's attitude rather than an employee attitude when speaking of work. At the end of a workday, the employee of a dress shop looks at the clock and says, "Five more minutes and I'm out of here." The owner of that same shop looks at that same clock and says, "Five minutes left. Think I'll stay an extra few minutes and put out that new line of sweaters in the back room before I leave. Some might sell if they're on the shelf tomorrow morning." I have taught both of my children the value of this saying, too. It gets you better grades, it gets just a bit more done every day, it earns you positive recognition at work, and it is a marvelous driver when playing sports.

In what other place would it eventually work for me? If you said dealing with cancer, you are really paying attention, and you are right. Doing those little extra things as a cancer patient to meet the daunting challenges is a powerful medicine—and it doesn't cause you to lose your hair. You know, it offsets that helpless feeling that could come over me at times before I realized I needed to reset my self-talk. *I wish I could do something.* Well, okay, Bantz, who's stopping you? If I did a little more than I thought I could when I was feeling sick, I found I did not feel as sick. In effect, that was the reset.

Through the years, as I came to better understand the power of self-talk, I acquired three corollaries to the common denominator of successful people. They are:

1. "Expect the best." Not only should we try to be our best, but we need to expect that of others also.
2. "The greatest danger for most of us is not that we aim too high and miss, but that we aim too low and reach it." —Michelangelo
3. "Finish strong." This one poignantly rings really true to a cancer patient.

Finish Strong

Number three, finish strong, has so many applications regarding my cancer. But I'm amazed to hear myself saying it very often, even in the simplest situations. I remember a major ending, retirement, when I knew finishing strong was important second only to my cancer experiences.

When I first told Derryck Jones, our best and final business partner, it was time for him to step in and take over and for me to retire, Derryck responded, "Dave, you have to stay at it longer. It's so obvious to others, especially our clients, how much you love what you do, and you've been successful, too." I did love the financial advisory business. Whenever asked by a client or acquaintance how long I had been in the business, I would say the number of years: ten, twenty, thirty, whatever it was at the time. But almost always, I would follow up by saying, "But it only feels like I've been doing this a couple of years. I can honestly say I have never been bored."

I stuck to my guns and tried to finish strong, knowing it was time. I responded to Derryck as we were arranging for him to take over our business during my thirty-third year, "I have always loved the business, Derryck; you're right. And you do, too. People can tell that with you, too. I believe Albert Schweitzer had it right when he said, 'Success is not the key to happiness. Happiness is the key to success.' If you love what you do, you will be successful." Happiness doing something is a strong incentive to do those things failures don't do. But I just knew it was time for me to finish strong and move on. Ironically, in 2010, just a month after I retired, I was told that I had cancer—again. I might have retired from my business, but who knew I would have my old job as cancer patient back?

Do More!

As you have read, I live in the San Diego area. I have been in the area since 1974. I also happen to be a sports fan of some consequence. Put those two facts together and you can guess that I have followed the San Diego Chargers football team and the San Diego Padres baseball team since I arrived. Over those decades, though the Padres have not won a World Series, they have had some good years and some truly great players.

I think many fellow Padres fans and most baseball fans would agree with me that the top Padre of all was Tony Gwynn, who played from 1982-2001. In fact, his nickname was Mr. Padre. By the time Tony retired, he had not only carried many of his fellow teammates on his back to postseason playoff opportunities; he had also accumulated a startling number of personal achievements all the while being a team player. During his career, he was a fifteen-time All-Star, and he won eight batting titles, tying for second most in baseball history, seven Silver Slugger Awards, and five Golden Glove Awards. He was inducted into the Baseball Hall of Fame in 2007.

Tony said the main reason he won those batting titles was he consistently spent just a little more time in the batting (practice) cage than any other team member almost every practice day. Tony said he knew batting titles are won by thousandths of a percentage point after many hundreds of at-bats through more than 160 games in a baseball year.

Clearly, he understood the messages here of doing just a little more than is expected every time, and successful people do the things failures don't like to do. He loved baseball, so he was doing what he loved and was doing it well, but to be as successful as he could be, he did more than less successful people did. You might call his approach "successful excellence." We also see this kind of extraordinary effort by Olympics participants.

Be Determined, and Show It

Though it may not seem so at times in the process of overcoming a cancer challenge, doctors are people, too (smile). As a boy, when I was worried about whether one of my friends liked me, my father asked me if I liked this friend. I answered quite quickly, "Well, yes." He said, "Then he probably likes you too, David." By this, he meant that most of the time, when someone likes us, we try to like them, too, if for no other reason than we want to confirm they are right to like us. This is simple self-talk that reassures. I have found this to be right and reassuring through the years.

If we like our doctors, chances are they like us, too. It has always seemed to me that my doctors were more committed to working with me during my cancer journey if they felt I liked them and was committed to my own healing, whether by surgery, chemo treatments, or other efforts. As in other experiences in my life, I had the feeling we were partners— remember, you'll see that word again—with our common goal of getting me well. I even told some of them that I felt they were partners. To a man and woman, they appreciated it.

I tried to convey my determination when discussing my case with the doctors I consulted. I also let my body do the talking. I tried to talk to doctors by minimizing signs of the tiredness I felt from the massive doses of chemo. I tried to demonstrate physical enthusiasm.

Dr. Alan Hemming, surgeon at UCSD's Moores Cancer Center, is part of the team of six doctors who were to save my life in 2010 by removing half my liver, most of the right side of my diaphragm, my gall bladder, and replacing part of my vena cava with a Gore-Tex hose—all within a month of our interview. Olivia and I went to see him toward the end of my chemo treatments by referral from both my San Diego oncologist and Dr. Andrew Lowy, who was the eventual lead surgeon for my case.

The "Job" Interview

Oh boy, do I remember that interview. I knew I was interviewing for my life, and I was determined to get the job. Just as in job interviews, each party is interviewing the other. I knew from several earlier rejections in which I had been deemed unsuitable for surgery that Dr. Hemming was interviewing me as much, and maybe more than, I was him. I felt I had to convey my willingness, determination, and enthusiasm for the surgery.

What a wonderful meeting it turned out to be. As Olivia and I walked to the consulting room, we walked past the nurses' station and I saw the back of a white coat studying MRIs on the screen. I knew that was my MRI. By this time, I could recognize my own insides. The white coat was really studying my charts and MRIs intently. His was deep in that information.

I remarked to Olivia, "Hey, Liv, that's me on the screen; that's our doctor!" We waited only a moment or two in the exam room. Then the door opened and Dr. Hemming said, "Mr. Bantz, you are kind of weird." I don't know why, but I came right back at him with a smile, saying, "Well,

Doctor, I think of myself as unusual." And we all laughed. His mind was obviously still locked on those "weird" MRIs, and with a wonderful smile, he then clarified that, of course, it was my case that was weird. He was stating the obvious; my case was weird. I told him I was excited and I couldn't resist making a little comeback. We had both immediately broken the ice. I have found humor is a valuable part of these tense medical life-and-death conversations. This was a terrific start.

As I mentioned in Chapter 1, people with my kind of cancer have an average survival rate of about two years after discovery. Life expectancy after five years is about 20 percent. They don't usually hang around for more than twenty-five years. But we ignored those statistics. His enthusiasm is still clear in Olivia's mind today. We all sat forward in our chairs as he went on to not only interview me, but also to be a great listener. He then began telling us how we could attack the problems created by such a large and tough surgical site with numerous organs involved. He even turned over the reports in his hand and began drawing sketches to help us understand the choices he would face at critical times during surgery. There was even a chance he might have to take my liver out of my body and put it in a dish of ice while he worked on it and then replace it. I later learned Dr. Hemming had done more than 900 liver surgeries in his career, frequently making these kinds of decisions in the process. Wow.

As the interview was coming to a conclusion, I was thrilled. He was the guy for us. I wanted him to know I felt that way. I said so with as much determination as I could in my weakened voice. I also wanted him to know I was still a tough, ready-for-action guy, even with the withered appearance of my body because of the disastrous effects of the chemo, which I felt were written all over me.

With my arms, I pushed myself into the air and jumped off the examination table as if I were doing a dismount from the parallel bars during my gymnastics days back in high school. *That'll show him I'm ready!* my self-talk said. Olivia and I still laugh at my antics. Hey, determination and enthusiasm went both ways that day, and we both landed the job.

Make Smart Choices

But back to my formative visit in Charleston, West Virginia, with Mr. Caperton. There's another lesson I had learned from interacting with Casey, even though I didn't realize it at the time. Not only did my meeting with Mr. Caperton plant wonderful seeds of self-talk; it was also to change the direction and the trajectory of my entire future. As we were wrapping up our conversation, shortly after Mr. Caperton had given me the little book and the pep talk on success, I remember him saying, "David, what are you doing about this war? Did you take ROTC in college?"

"No, sir." I responded as firmly as I could, but I heard my voice wavering anyway. He was a tall, somewhat stern-looking man, much taller than I, and I remember him looking down his long nose toward me and saying, "Oh, dear."

He thought a moment and then said, "Have you ever considered being in the navy rather than being in the army?"

"No, sir," I said again. With growing embarrassment, I continued, "You know, sir, I haven't really thought about the military at all."

Mr. Caperton, in his best fatherly voice, said without hesitation, "Well, son, they're thinking about you. I'm going to talk to your mother and have her sign you up for a test. If you pass that test, you'll be going into navy officer training. It's known as OCS, Officer Candidate School. If you make it through that program, you'll be a navy officer rather than an Aamy private—and son, there's a very big difference between the two right now. God bless you. Let's go talk to your mother."

That meeting was obviously pivotal in my life. First, Mr. Caperton had succinctly defined success and how to be successful in a way that stuck with me. Secondly, Casey and Mr. Caperton may have saved my life by redirecting me to a navy officer's service rather than that of a private who likely would have been sent into the jungles of Vietnam. Casey had wisely put me in contact with a kind and knowledgeable friend who also had a son. She knew I (we) would get the truly sage advice from this man that she wasn't capable of giving me. And she knew by now I was a youngster who would listen.

I was learning from Casey and employing that knowledge simultaneously. Now I hope I can make my experience just as meaningful for you. There is My Chi here. Rather than get "socked with the draft," as we used to say back then, I chose to accept the reality of military service but then take control—in My Chi parlance—to surrender to a stronger position and do it on my terms.

Because of Casey's and Mr. Caperton's clear observations that I had a choice, I saw the "punch" of the draft into military service coming at me. However, they coached me to move aside and use the force of that punch and redirect it to regain control of my life path. Not being politically active at the time, nor being a conscientious objector, a strategy of avoidance was not in the cards. And I would not be a draft dodger—just not my nature. So it was a given that I would willingly, enthusiastically serve my country. However, I would determine and choose (there's that word again) how I would serve. I regained control of my life. I, not the government, would determine how I would serve, as a new, very young navy officer.

CHAPTER 11

ACTIONS HAVE CONSEQUENCES

When one body exerts a force on a second body, the second body simultaneously exerts a force equal in magnitude and opposite in direction on the first body.

—Sir Isaac Newton, 1687

Obstacles are those frightful things you see when you take your eyes off your goals.

—Henry Ford

Big, simplistic picture: life is basically a series of tens of millions of choices. Some easier than others, some incredibly tough, but all must be made. Life is all about greeting those moments requiring decisions as challenges, especially when we start off a sequence making the wrong choice and must self-correct. Our self-talk must not waver. We are all continually challenged to overcome obstacles in our lives. Time again to self-talk of my favorite sayings.

Establishing Goals

Establishing goals gives you a reason to make a series of decisions with meaning or intent. A lot of people think it was Yogi Berra, but it was English author Lewis Carroll who first said, "If you don't know where you are going, any road will get you there." Regardless of the source, it is a truism. And the reverse is true. If you establish a goal, even though you may not think you are working on it, you will find you are getting closer to that goal every day. Set goals and you will know where you are going—and you will get there. Actions can have wonderful consequences if you have goals in mind.

Studies show we make nearly 50,000 self-talk comments a day. We make many millions of decisions as we proceed through our lives. I think our creator has a mischievous sense of humor in that s/he constantly invents new ways for us with our human characteristic of self-determination to have to respond. Every day, we have that chance to make the correct or incorrect decision for ourselves and others. Just because we have failed in the past (and at times, we all have), that does not color anything but our self-talk about our ability to get the response to the next challenge right.

An astute and sometimes controversial psychologist and talk show host, Dr. Laura Schlessinger, has a daily call-in-for-help talk show. As she finishes her response to a question about what to do about a caller's dilemma, such as a cheating spouse or how to manage any number of tough life situations where mistakes were made, she often goes to commercial with "Now, go do the right thing!" Good advice.

$$E + R = O$$

E stands for Event, R is your response. And O is the outcome.

Jack Canfield, whom I mentioned earlier and wrote *Chicken Soup for the Soul,* among many other books, created this equation. Canfield gave an example of this equation I have found very valuable. I paraphrase his commentary in the following: if a lady in your office is late almost every day and she says, "It was the traffic. It was horrible today," each day when she is late, it doesn't take long to determine that there is a problem, and it's not the traffic. The bad traffic is the event (E). The outcome (O) is she is late. But this is a constant occurrence. What is her response (R)? At what point does she change her response? After the first couple of days, she knows the traffic will be bad, therefore don't you think she needs to leave a bit earlier? Somewhere in here, there has to be logic. Being late is an unattractive trait in a person. Importantly, it is disrespectful of other people's most valuable asset: their time. This lady is at a minimum irritating her coworkers and maybe eventually putting her job on the line if cuts have to be made in staff.

Actions have consequences. Seeds are planted. Events occur. What is the outcome? There is no way to answer that until we find out what our human action was in response to the event. I believe it can change outcomes in people's lives if they apply this equation consistently and positively as a test of the quality of their behavior in various situations.

E+R=O. It's simple, but how many examples of questionable responses can you cite in the next week as you spend time with others? Maybe you can even summon the courage to try to form the habit of evaluating your own responses to events. We have a choice in how we respond. Over time, the quality of that response will determine the quality of our lives.

When Events occur, let your self-talk help you to make the right Response to achieve the best Outcomes in your daily life.

A Paradox, Counterintuitive, or Both?

Actions have consequences counterintuitively, as well. Think about this. The more responsibility you take, the more freedom you gain. This is something that echoes in my children's ears. This is true whether creating trust in your parents' or your boss's mind later in life. If we create trust by consistently acting in a responsible way, others who might have control of a part of our lives will give us more personal freedom to manage our own lives. I find so much of life is counterintuitive. This is a just fact of life, but few seem to understand this paradox or counterintuitive fact in this day and age.

A concept related to the idea that taking more responsibility begets more freedom is training your mind to think two or three steps ahead. When we play checkers or chess, the game is about seeing the whole board and building a strategy to be successful three moves from now, not on the next move. Each move has a consequence that will affect the final consequence but not necessarily *be* the final consequence. These games are a micro view of life. If people don't learn to think many steps ahead in their lives, there will be consequences, and they will most likely be negative. A prime example here would be not planning and saving for retirement.

Today, our children play *Angry Birds* or some military first-person shooting game like *Call of Duty*, where we react to the next thing popping on the screen. Then there's e-mail and Twitter, where people are saying the next thing on their minds rather than thinking about the longer impact of those words, when they might be viewed later by a prospective employer. With the modern pace of life, people seem to do much less long-term strategic thinking. We watch television with fifteen-second commercials flashing by and see people on reality and competition shows like *American Idol* as examples of success. They become singing stars or sports personalities seemingly overnight. Who among your friends plays chess or checkers these days? Who among your friends can you identify as being a strategic thinker? It's surprising how few, is it not?

Speaking of games, you know by now I am a golf fan and a golfer. When golfers are on the course, two major actions affect their quality of play. Of course, the physical prowess they bring to the game is critical. Each golfer has his or her natural abilities, and each makes choices about how much to hone those skills with practice. The other is not so obvious, but professional or amateur, we win or lose games because of the quality of our course management.

The term *course management,* as I mentioned before, is used by golfers to encompass the totality of all the decisions a player makes while on the course during play. Events such as being behind a tree and the decisions—Responses—we make have outcomes that separate winners from losers in golf and life in general. Yes, even in golf, E+R=O matters. The player who chips out to the fairway safely knows the damage from the previous shot that ended up behind the tree is limited to the one stroke. But the player who takes the additional risk of going over or under the tree trying to avoid the extra stroke caused by the first error may take even more strokes if he doesn't make the difficult shot. He may be making a bad situation worse.

Thinking Three Steps ahead with Cancer

I found these concepts—every action has a consequence and training your mind to think steps ahead, including forming goals—to be imperative when responding to my cancer challenges. Cancer is big. It seemed overwhelming as it stormed into my life again and again. There seemed nowhere to hide, and fear found fertile ground. There was no one-step solution. Rather than remain fearful and overwhelmed, which I admit I have been temporarily each time my cancer has occurred, my wife and I had to calm ourselves and break down the tasks we suddenly had to put at the top of our list of things to do.

An inch is a cinch. A mile is a trial. It's a cute cliché, but it holds up after the cute factor fades. Doing the little things, setting short-term goals like placing phone calls and achieving them, was critical to getting the larger results of lining up doctor's appointments and finally arriving at solutions we felt gave me the best chance for survival. I found achieving those little goals was calming. Inevitably, with time, Olivia and I were experiencing the big returns from having thought several moves ahead. If you are currently dealing with "miles" of cancer, break your assignments down to "inches" of small, achievable goals that you know will get you to your best outcome, whatever that might be.

And Raising Children

My wife's brother, Richard, is a smart guy and an even smarter parent. One day, my wife picked up the phone and found he was more than a bit perturbed. That's unusual for him. He had traveled all the way from St. Louis to Florida to take his son to a baseball camp. That's a nice gesture by a dedicated dad of a successful high school kid in academics and sports. He was moving his son's experience from good to great by helping his son learn to do the things that failures didn't do. It also looked like it could be a memorable dad-and-son trip.

But Richard was unhappy when he called because, at that moment, he was driving back to the airport to get his son's duffle bag of sports gear. Sam had looked back into the car as he got out at the stadium and said,

"Uh, Dad, could you please go back to the airport and get my bag for me?" Richard was on his way back when my wife picked up the phone, and he let off a little steam as he spoke to us. "Kids these days!" he said, as all parents have. "They have to learn that actions have consequences!" What a great, succinct statement: actions have consequences. And it fits in so well with the common denominator of success: successes do the things failures don't like to do.

Yes, actions do have consequences, and at this time in our country's history, I join my brother-in-law in this thought as I sometimes shake my head in amazement that not only kids, but also grown-ups seem not to be making that connection. Call it destiny, call it karma, whatever you name it, the fact is, if you do something—or correspondingly, do *not* do something—there will be something or someone else who is affected. Note, there is no value judgment, and there are no politics in that statement. This is a truism we must live with whether good or bad repercussions result. In this case, Richard had to race back to the airport. I knew this would be a teaching moment for his son that would maybe make a big impact.

Seeds Are Planted

I told a friend this story, and we began looking at the ways different friends' lives had unfolded. He asked me if I could come up with a seemingly small moment that spurred action on my part that became truly consequential. Being a fundamental optimist, I thought of a unique, seemingly small moment that gave me a big kick in a different direction I had never knowingly contemplated before.

I explained to him that experiencing the loss of my parents so early, even with my stepmother's arrival in my life, created striking gaps in my knowledge of some seemingly obvious things. In truth, I was quite naïve in certain areas. The example I gave to him was somewhat embarrassing, but that made it all the more significant to me. I told him I could remember the moment, just out of the navy at age twenty-six, when I was walking along looking at the huge buildings on each side of K Street in Washington, DC, and had a flash of realization. I found my self-talk saying, "Wow, people actually own these huge buildings."

It was a grown-up version of the shock of finding out there is no Santa Claus or the feeling I had when I realized Chubby Checker (singer of the song "The Twist" in the early 1960s) had actually built his name off of another very popular singer, Fats Domino (I found my thrill on "Blueberry Hill"). I felt silly but also strangely pleased that I hadn't realized this economic reality before. I self-talked my amazement. How about that? It turned out this shocking realization would be a lot bigger for me than Santa or Chubby.

For me, seeing those buildings in such a different way was a signature moment; it was a real revelation because in my teens, I had not been exposed to the world of business in any way. I had a frightfully busy dad who wasn't able to spend a lot of relaxed/chatty time with me. He worked with the nonprofit YMCA, so the concepts of business ownership, earnings, cash flow and profits never came up between us. That lack of interaction had a consequence.

In addition, as my stepmom helped me through college with the insurance money that resulted after my dad died, I worked every summer, but in menial, nonbusiness jobs. I was a janitor in a steel mill in Columbus, Ohio. The next summer, I landed the job of an all-around gardener/gofer on a large estate in Westport, Connecticut. I found both of those jobs while spending the summer with fraternity brothers. The closest I got to business experience was selling men's clothing in a Charleston, West Virginia, department store the one summer I spent home with my stepmom.

I only took these jobs trying to find a way to supplement her generosity, not as any kind of internship. In other words, I had no exposure to and did not understand business or entrepreneurism. I wasn't building useful job references or experience of any kind, because I had no idea what I wanted to do other than get out of college. As I mentioned, I even majored in sociology, for goodness sake! See what I mean? And those actions of general nondirection were to have painful consequences later when I had real trouble landing a job after my four years as an officer in the navy.

Admiral Francis Foley bestowing my promotion

During my navy service, onboard the ship one day, way out at sea in the Pacific Ocean, the executive officer and the captain were talking in my presence. I was the officer of the deck on a four-hour shift. That meant I was supposed to be paying attention to the movement of my ship, the radar screens, all things going on in the sea around us, and everything happening onboard for four long hours. At sea, there is often nothing going on, nothing to look at except the long, thin blue line that stretches all the way around the ship across the horizon—because it is the horizon. That's it. That's all we could see, 360 degrees around us.

So I couldn't help hearing my two senior officers talk of the stock market and companies and shares. It sounded intriguing, so, knowing it never hurts to ask, I asked a few questions. They tried to explain a couple business concepts to me about ownership and profits and earnings. The answers flew high over my head at the time. But I did file the experience away. They had planted the seed, and the full recollection of the captain's kind instructions about capitalism popped up as I looked at the buildings on K Street.

I came to a full stop. *Wham!* My self-talk blurted out, "That's it! I have to get involved in that!" From that moment, I began soaking up all I could about business and what an entrepreneur was. I loved it.

Before long, I interviewed for a job at a financial services brokerage office in midtown Washington, DC. The resume looked pretty good on paper and over the phone: Wake Forest College graduate, navy officer for four years, including two promotions with excellent fitness reports (performance reviews), now working at a small publishing firm owned by sister while interviewing. But when I walked in and the resident manager took one look at my baby face and short stature, he gently said, "Son, you are definitely a candidate for this position on paper, only not for another four or five years. Nobody in their fifties or sixties is going to give you their money to manage. I wish you good luck, and I mean it. Come back in three or four years." What a disappointment. But a positive consequence occurred because of how I chose to interpret what had happened. "All partial evil, universal good" came to my mind later that night. I would do the next thing I could.

I was determined to join that industry. My self-talk said, "Keep on keepin' on." The chess-game analogy applies here. I developed a series of short-term moves/goals that would end up landing me the job I wanted. It started with a small step. I took a night course in accounting at American University. (Can you imagine that? The kid with the twenty-eight undone math assignments takes a college course in accounting.) That A+ set me up to go after the complete MBA in finance, which prepared me to land a job three years later—just about like the manager said—at a brokerage office and to create a career in that industry over the next thirty-three years.

I'm proud to say that self-talk aphorisms "actions have consequences;" and "successful people do the things that failures don't want to do;" and "keep on keepin' on" were my constant companions. I stuck with them in some tough times during those years, and so did my new wife, Lori. We prevailed. I landed my position as a financial advisor in San Diego even before I completed my MBA program at University of San Diego.

Checkmate. I win.

CHAPTER 12

I CAN SEE CLEARLY NOW

Prediction is very difficult, especially if it is about the future.
—Nils Bohr, Nobel Laureate in physics

I gained strength to deal with the continual returns of my cancer from my early years in a strange way that was not obvious at the time. In fact, the deaths of both my mother and father before I was a senior in high school seemed a terrible thing. My faith was challenged early in my life, and my abilities to deal with adversity were tested and strengthened immeasurably. While these tragedies were destabilizing in the short term, I did have the benefit of a stepmom who stood by me through the loss of my dad rather than deserting me.

Casey—Stepmom and Partner

As you know from reading earlier chapters, Casey, my new stepmom and a very savvy and smart woman, found out upon her arrival with us that I was twenty-eight homework assignments behind in my ninth-grade math class and in trouble in several other subjects. I think back and I marvel at how gracefully she accepted me and quietly made me her project. But she also knew our home life with my dad could be better, too.

She actually "managed" our futures and my decision to go south to college. I didn't know this then, nor did she, but as I think back now, this was a version of applying t'ai chi (My Chi) principles to interpersonal

98

relationships. It was natural for Casey. She was using *my* energy as she stepped out of the way and "pulled me through" changing our home attitude and managing the college decision-making process. All this time, without realizing it, I was learning from her and was improving those personal skills my original Mom had seen in her little diplomat.

The Pact

One Saturday afternoon, after a minor family squabble, Casey asked me to join her on our front steps. My dad was having a bad day worrying about several things and demonstrating these worries to us, if you know what I mean. Unfortunately, he was good at these demonstrations, and I was learning from him very well how to do them, too. She definitely did not want my father's short-term, snarly bad acting to continue and take hold in me, too. So after some casual talk, Casey looked right at me and said, "David, let's team up and make a pact." I responded, "Okay, what?" I was willing to do anything to please her. By now, I knew she was just wonderful to and for my dad and me. She said, "Let's make these future years for your dad the most wonderful he could possibly imagine."

The Partnership

I was already smitten. Now I was completely over the edge, and I immediately said, "That's a wonderful pact!" with as big a smile as I'd had in years. After this front-porch talk, she and I began making eye contact whenever my dad was unhappy, and together as partners, we would cooperate to redirect his focus and turn his attitude around.

Instead of my being another problem, she had performed a mental t'ai chi move on me. She had pulled me into her "empty space" alongside her and taken control. Instead of her having to deal with possible bad antics from me and my dad, in one pleasant gesture, she had subtly identified for me what my dad was doing and used my energy along with hers to affect my dad's and my behavior positively. After Casey's wonderful way of bringing me in by offering to be partners to create happiness for my dad, let's just say she had my attention.

Inspired and now feeling her love and support, my grades shot up to As and Bs, and I became involved in all sorts of sports and extracurricular activities for the next three years. I even attempted being a rock-and-roll singer in our school play imitation of the popular *Dick Clark Show,* as you can see below.

We kept our pact, and for the next three years, Casey and my father and I had a fantastic time together. My dad, much as he loved my first mom, never had such a great time as he did with Casey. If our family had been a boat, her presence and actions were like a deep keel cutting through the rough ocean of life that my dad and I had been weathering. Everything became calmer, and we were now on a steady course.

But as you know, my dad died suddenly at age fifty-six in the summer before my senior year. I was only sixteen, and on that warm night in June 1961, out of nowhere, we were challenged to our core. His death was caused by a massive stroke from a clot in his brain. We had gone to bed on a lovely midsummer night as a happy threesome having the time of our lives.

Blinding Snowstorm

Within days, my dad was dead, and Casey's and my vision of our future was the same as that of a driver in a blinding snowstorm on the New York State Thruway: visibility zero. That vision is what came to my mind after my dad died, and I knew why. Years earlier, my dad had scrambled his little eleven-year-old boy into his car late one winter night in upstate New York and said, "Davey, get in; we are going to New York City!" I said, "But Dad, it's snowing really hard." All he said was, "Son, your mother is in New York City, and she needs us." The truth was she had been undergoing another one of the terrible cobalt treatments for her uterine cancer. She had endured these horrific, now defunct forms of treatment for the last several years and had not come away from this most recent one well. Dad knew she was at death's door. He was wound tight as a drum. He could get that way, and this was one of those times. I was really scared.

Even now, I remember so vividly looking through the windshield of our car as we raced through the night, windshield wipers making a loud *flap-flap* noise as they whipped back and forth. From a boy's angle in the passenger seat, I was seeing total blackness with millions of bright-white snowflakes zooming at us in the headlights. How my dad was driving in this blinding storm on the New York State Thruway, I didn't know. Now I was unbelievably scared.

Fast forward, as I contemplated my dad's death, I again saw those white flakes flying through the black in my mind. My future was visibility zero again. It was just as unknown as when Dad and I were racing to New York City. Now, even with wonderful Casey in my life, I knew my future was … what?

Here we were, a fifty-five-year-old twice widowed lady with a sixteen-year-old boy in tow. We could not see our futures past our arms' lengths. One of her friends came into the living room at the reception after my dad's funeral and said, "Oh, Casey! Again!" I have never forgotten that moment and how it made me feel for her. She had already lost a husband in her forties. And now my dad was gone, and she only had three years with him. My consolation was I knew we had given my dad the best three years in his life, and I felt that Casey probably felt that way herself.

But what about our futures? Casey was so graceful in the way she managed that time. She was magnificent in her strength. It almost seemed she was consoling her friends rather than the other way around, as they came through the door with food and all sorts of things they thought might help us in the short term. She made it so clear to me that I was not alone during those times. I wished a sixteen-year-old had the power to console a fifty-five-year-old, but the odds were against me.

She did later say that I really was part of her strength. I remember crying inconsolably only once during the ordeal. It was in the hall outside my dad's hospital room when they told me he was gone. But she said not only did I "hold myself together" through that time, but also I immediately became a reason for her to maintain herself through those tough times and lead me by example. She said I responded admirably. I hope so. Today, as I look back, my feelings the first few days after Dad's death are just a blur. I think after that explosive cry, I was just numb, but I guess I was well behaved in my numbness.

Then came an incredible moment in late June. We were at breakfast when light poured into my world and my future cracked wide open because of her grace and kindness. Casey announced to me that she would not move us back to Charleston, which had been her home for years before moving to marry my dad. She would delay the move and stay in Schenectady, New York, for my next school year. It was my senior year in high school, and she realized how important that year would be for me. Even though I am sure I was appreciative, I could not have seen at age sixteen what I now see clearly from age seventy. What a gift this was, and given without expectation, just empathy for my situation and, yes, grace.

My Chi

Also, I now see there was My Chi in her decision and my reactions. She was backing away or, in My Chi terms, surrendering by letting me stay for my senior year. She knew by taking what could be viewed as a short-term surrender or "loss" of not being able to spend the next year back in her former hometown, she would put herself (and therefore me) in a "superior" position longer term and create a big win for both of us. My

Chi reasoning can be such a beautiful blend of having presence of mind, good judgment, and empathy. And using My Chi to manage a situation can create a willingness by the other person involved to partner to achieve common goals.

I now see this was my motivation to partner with my stepmom back then. I, too, yielded or surrendered and accepted her direction rather than fighting with her. My self-talk had switched from negative to positive as my school experience dramatically improved. That positive thinking allowed me to readily accept the "good," and Pope's words were encouraging me to look for that good through all the terrible "partial evil" and sadness of having lost my mom and now my dad so shockingly early.

It was my positive self-talk that kept me focused on the good. I powered through the sadness by focusing on what Casey and I together could do about the future. I was looking at the present and forward for a way to resurrect the good from these terrible events rather than be dragged down by constantly looking back at them.

From my adolescent perspective and relying on Pope's message in his essay, my "partial evil" began almost miraculously turning to good in my universe. I was looking for something good, and new stepmom/partner Casey turned out to be part of that good. Thank God, first of all, that I was looking for the good and then that I chose to accept her rather than fight her entry into my dad's and my life.

I marvel at this overarching pattern of rolling good and evil we all have in our lives. Knowing this pattern exists instills and maintains my faith when bad times occur. I know if I can only keep looking for the eventual good, I will recognize it for what it is when I see it and then trust it. Managing our self-talk by quickly resetting when it is knocked off track by sad and evil events is a sure way to stay focused and, if not happy at the moment, at least positive and looking for the good to reappear.

In this instance, my search for good and my faith were rewarded. I was inspired by her gift and wanted to please Casey more than ever. I leapt into the space she offered in the form of my senior year in high school. I hammered my schoolwork and got the best grades I could. More than that, I busied myself playing team sports, including soccer and volleyball. I pole vaulted for the track team and became a member of the student council, Key Club, and Ski Club. I had my first "beyond-puppy-love" girlfriend, Sharon, with whom I still correspond and about whom I still think wonderful things. We both savor the memories we created.

In other words, I had a great senior year. This thrilled Casey. We were partners still, even without my dad. Through her unknowing but natural use of My Chi, she had offered a gift that changed my senior year, and I had responded with a gift of my own to her: I did well in school.

During the winter of that senior year, Casey offered another gift that would again significantly alter the trajectory of my life. She said she would use as much of my dad's life insurance as I needed to put me through four years of college. To implement this college effort, we were going to take a college tour to help me choose a school. As I look back, I see this was such artful use of My Chi.

Some parents and others in leadership positions use discipline and the word *no* or "You *will* …" and exercise their supposed superiority or authority in this kind of situation. Casey could have said, "I'm moving back to the south, so you're going south to college, David." I probably would have responded like so many other teenagers in that situation: "No, I'm old enough now to make my own decision, and I want to go to the University of Vermont to try out for the ski team."

No doubt a battle of stubborn wills would have ensued, with hurt feelings and unhappiness being the baggage we carried forward. But instead, Casey suggested we go on a college tour to see several schools in the south. She let our on-site tours do the talking and encouraged me to express positive and negative reviews in the car as we drove from one school campus to the next during the trip to the south that week. Naturally, by engaging me, she had her chance to voice her opinions, too and bent the conversations continually toward my choice being one of the schools in the south. Perfect My Chi.

Casey did not rule. She led me by showing me various possibilities and alternatives to my first thought. She engaged me, drew me into discussions, and reasoned with me. She led me forward rather than telling me what I was to do or putting barriers in my way. It was a great college search trip. Wake Forest has a beautiful campus, and I had a wonderful interview with Dr. Gene Starling, then director of admissions. Back then and certainly now, I didn't really have the grades to qualify for Wake Forest (also affectionately known by students as Work Forest). But all the activities and sports, and especially the interview I had with Dr. Starling, must have made the difference. Casey and I had done it again, with My Chi-like positive leadership and her grace. I was also accepted at the University of Vermont, where I could have skied, but I chose Wake.

The next year, as I happily went off to college at Wake Forest in Winston-Salem, North Carolina, Casey moved back to her hometown, Charleston, West Virginia. This is where she had lived many years before marrying my dad. It was only four hours by car from Wake. She was again in the comfort of her former home among her best long-term friends. We were both Southerners now, and just a little more than one year after my dad's death, we both had futures again.

Create Your Future

Years later, in my late twenties, while studying for my graduate degree, I found an aphorism that reminded me of her efforts back then. Business professor and renowned author Peter Drucker once said, "The best way to predict the future is to create it."

I realized my stepmom had been taking that kind of creative action and intuitively used My Chi. She had predicted our future by creating it for us back then.

To me, Drucker's phrase implies overt action. It is therefore very empowering. Act, don't react. So, during my early working years, I made a sign with this phrase on it and put it in the center of my desk at my office. It became for me a spur to help my clients create their futures, just as Casey and I had for ourselves. It was there on my desk for more than twenty-five years. Years later, in my early forties and facing cancer, I put another sign right next to the Drucker statement. It was a gift my daughter gave me when she was in her early teens. It was part of her way of helping me deal with my first cancer challenge. I loved her fearless, loving gesture and also felt like it was another reminder that fit well with Drucker's. In big letters, it said:

Determination.

Casey wasn't confronting me or blocking my potential teenage contrariness. She was managing me so beautifully that even though I sometimes sensed she was, I loved it. This is true leadership of the highest order to identify and deliver this style of leadership. She set a high bar for me as I tried to establish my own way of living with others later in my life.

CHAPTER 13

SO SHOW ME

The cynical attitude exerts an influence on its environment
not unlike that of acid; it cuts through … it destroys.
—Shepherd Hoodwin

Skeptics versus Cynics

Some people believe there is a happy gene. But that is not what we will
be discussing here. Positive self-talk and being a skeptic rather than a cynic
can be learned behaviors. I believe cynicism is a habit—a destructive one.
It can be unlearned. Be a happy skeptic for a day, and with every problem
that pops up, use your self-talk and ask yourself to consider it a challenge
or an opportunity instead of a problem. Say to yourself, "Where are the
opportunities in this situation?" It's liberating.

To paraphrase Eleanor Roosevelt, a stumbling block to a cynic is a
building block to the skeptic.

Some artists and creative types use naiveté to activate their muse, but
none of us aspires to be naïve in the way we run our lives, right? As we grow
up, most of us hope to learn to be discerning decision-makers. That means
we have to learn to question people and things in our lives effectively. But
over the long term, the attitude we use in developing and employing those
questioning skills may have a profound effect on our overriding successes
and relationships.

Let's start with a couple of definitions:

Skeptic: One who has a doubting attitude toward plans and other people's statements. One who has reservations about new ideas but may be convinced over time.

Cynic: One who is critical of the motives of others and has a generally negative, bitter, or unhappy outlook on many matters in life. One who believes the worst in people and maintains that view, even in the face of contrary evidence.

Simply put, skeptics look for holes in your idea because they want to help you plug those holes. Cynics look for holes so they can make them bigger and sink your idea.

Actually, they both sound unattractive, don't they? But notice that part of the definition of a cynic includes *negative* and *bitter*. I am proud to call myself a self-trained skeptic. Here's a story encasing the moment that sensitized me to the choices in this paradigm.

As the resident rookie, I walked through the brokerage office to my cubicle one day in 1976 and I remember saying to myself about a co-worker, "Wow, no wonder he doesn't do the business Dan does." Roger was a technically brilliant guy in our business and talked all the time with other brokers in the office about his market observations. For a while, I really respected him for his knowledge. But as the months went by, I noticed a clearly negative point of view that pervaded his offerings.

Roger usually ended up emphasizing a negative within his presentation, not the potential opportunities that might coexist with the challenges. It was almost as if he didn't believe in his take on the markets or his ability to interpret them in a way that benefited him or his clients. If the market was selling off, he was not realizing that the lower prices could be a buying opportunity longer term for his clients. Instead, he was saying how much danger was involved and that it might fall further. When the market shot up, it was "too high" to dare buy in because of the possibility of a sell-off. He would say things like, "The guys on the floor are trying to suck us in with this rally."

I found myself thinking things like, *Well, okay, but you must have some clients who need to do a little selling;* or, *Good grief, go get some air. It's a beautiful day outside.* As I first became aware of this pattern, I thought he was just being cautious. But then I realized that, even as smart and well-schooled as he was, he did very little business. He was so cynical he was talking himself out of it.

Dan, on the other hand, was always looking for opportunity in the overall market's short-term moves. He was no smarter than Roger, maybe even a little less tuned in to the market. Nor was he a Pollyanna. He did carry a skeptical, analytical, but clearly happy view of the markets, believing he could help his clients. Slowly but surely, he was building a large book of very happy clients—like him. Intrigued, I decided to gently find out more about Roger's business.

Over time, I found out it had been stalled for years. Roger had attracted a book of clients who had the same cynical, nonbelieving attitudes about the financial markets and just about everything and everyone else in their lives. Dan was gaining and imparting wisdom. Roger was becoming increasingly cynical, thereby confirming his view and becoming a sad fellow.

I moved on to another firm and lost touch with Roger and Dan over time, although I ran into Dan at a conference about four years after our departures, and we happily shared our successes for a few moments. I thought of Roger later on that evening and wondered with some trepidation how he was. I realized this was an example of how we attract people around us over the years whose outlook is not too different from ours. Since then, I have seen many Rogers, the cynics in my life's path. I try my best to avoid them. You have heard the admonition to "avoid toxic people." Good advice. The skeptics and I have a great time trying to find opportunities in our problems and develop strengths from the challenges.

Apparently, Oscar Wilde knew people like Roger, too. In 1892, in "Lady Windermere's Fan," he wrote: "What is a cynic? A man who knows the price of everything and the value of nothing.

The Friendly Skeptic with Doctors

When I talked with my doctors, I tried my very best to remain open-minded and pay attention, i.e., a friendly skeptic. My life was in the balance. For me, because of the disappointment of having cancer (again), I could feel how easy it was to focus only on myself and not consider the doctor's circumstances and thoughts. I tried to have a friendly, gentle sort of paranoia, also known as empathy. This was not easy when thoughts were racing through my mind about my mortality. But, My Chi-like, I knew the doctor would relate to me better if I made the conscious effort to relate to him.

The more attention I paid to many of my doctors, the more they seemed to focus in and be concerned about my well-being. I was not going to be a deflated cynic, no matter how unhappy I was about my current circumstance. "The more you give, the more you get," applies in so many areas of our lives. While this is a concept somewhat easy to understand, it is very hard to execute when under life's pressures.

Focused self-talk before appointments and, of course, during appointments, directed at achieving this empathetic relationship with the doctor is not unlike a promise to oneself to act better when trying to relate to a disturbing person in other parts of life, someone who can irritate you. This person can be in the office, especially a senior person, a neighbor, or a love interest or relative.

The Problem or the Solution

Just recently, I discovered a profundity—at least, it was for me. Sometimes when we see a challenge and it doesn't seem to go away or be resolvable, we have to ask ourselves through our self-talk, "Am I the part of the problem, not the solution?"

When it happens, am I strong enough to admit that to others? Olivia, my wife, has a daughter by her first marriage who is now in her forties. They have always had "issues," as we say in the current parlance. As the interloper years ago into an already complicated relationship, I, the new husband, seemed to be the one to get in trouble if I made an attempt to referee or if I commented on their relationship without being asked. This had been the case for years.

One weekend, Petra, Olivia's daughter, came to visit. The weekend had gone so well, Olivia and I were pinching ourselves. But it seemed Petra was not focused at all on planning her departure. So, during a moment when we were alone, I asked Olivia when she thought Petra would be leaving. Uh oh. I think I had a bit of a cynical edge in my voice implying I was beginning to hope it was soon, and Olivia heard it. Because Olivia thought I was pushing, soon after I was out of earshot, *kaboom!* Petra went flying through the house toward her room. Olivia had asked, point blank, "When are you leaving?"

I thought about what just happened. In this instance, they were not the problem, I was. I should have known Olivia would be sensitive to my question, and so I had created the dynamic. They hadn't. I went to Petra. I told her we were having a lovely time with her visit. I told her, however, she had a choice of whether it continued, and her mother and I did not. She could calm herself and forgive her mother and return to the patio outdoors or she could continue slamming things around and leave in a huff. I told her we didn't want her to leave, but it was her choice. Neither her mother nor I could do anything to change the course of her actions.

We ended up in a huge hug with a few tears, and I was amazed when she returned to the room and enjoyed the rest of the day with us. I admitted to myself that I had created the situation, maybe even on purpose. I was the problem. I had to be the one to resolve it. Letting Petra know directly how I felt, not through her mother, was my courageous act for the day. I went from being a bit of a sneaky cynic back to being a happy skeptic with that act. And the weekend ended later that day on a happy, peaceful, loving note. Two weekends later, Petra came to our home again and we had a great time. Hmmm. I think I'm on to something here.

Skeptics in High Places

One of the most effective skeptics in our recent political history was President Ronald Reagan. I say this regardless of my political persuasion, because it undeniably shows in many of his speeches. Possibly the most well-known moment when he showed his happy but skeptical approach was when he told the world and Mr. Gorbachev he intended to work with the USSR regarding nuclear negotiations. However, his method would be that of "trust but verify." Yes, he saw the risks, but he also wanted to take full advantage of the opportunities.

An unlikely high place (not that of a political office, however) also yields many examples of the peril of the cynic as opposed to the benefits of being a skeptic. Since I'm a golfer, I see many moments of cynic versus skeptic. The elevated tee box on the eleventh hole at my local course is on what golfers call a water hole, in that it has a big pond right in the center front of our view. That's the high place where cynicism and negative self-talk bloom on this course.

So many times, I have heard someone in a foursome say, "Oh man, I hate water holes. I always hit it in the water." And as mentioned in a previous chapter, the brain doesn't differentiate a negative command; it just hears *water*. You're getting it: that's a cynical self-talk response to a challenge, and the golfer has set himself up for failure. The skeptical golfer sees the water and might say, "After I clear that water and land on the fairway, this is an easy par five." Or he sees a tree as a target in the distance and says, "I want to hit right at that tree in the distance."

We have about twelve guys who play together when we are available, and one of them is a recent addition. He lost his wife about three years ago and went into a bit of seclusion. He's fundamentally a very nice guy, and we are happy to have him back on the course with us. But we have had to resolve among the group without his knowing that we intend to help him out of what appears to be a cynical funk.

He became angry at himself for every less-than-great shot and negative and cynical from the first hole to the eighteenth his first time back with us since his wife died. We didn't even like to ride in the same cart with him at first. But now we think we have helped him turn himself around with laughter and by modeling a different way of approaching the course and the game. The cynicism has disappeared, and the happy skeptic is on the rise. He's playing better, too. In a bit of turnabout, I recently rode in the same cart with him, and he was calmer than I when we had a bad hole. I had to hit the reset button several times during the round. We're always learning.

Hanging out with or partnering with other happy skeptics can help us through all sorts of tough times, including losing loved ones or even contracting cancer. I know. I've done both. Now, every day, I give thanks to my great, happy, skeptical friends all along the way.

CHAPTER 14

GET A LIFE! (FORGIVENESS)

If you can't forgive and forget, pick one.

—Robert Brault

Forgiveness fits perfectly into my use of self-talk and the reset idea. It did especially during my most recent cancer days.

Part of what we cancer patients do after diagnosis is to recalibrate things in our lives with this new knowledge we have. If we have a serious cancer, perhaps a late stage or some other incurable condition, we may *know* about how long we have left on this earth. When we first get this news, there is no other way to look at it than as really bad news. But after the shock, the resilience of the human spirit has an amazing effect on some of us. We can choose to use this knowledge in positive ways.

For me, I have "known" how long I have left four times. All four of those moments, when I heard a sentence starting off with, "Dave, we have a bit of bad news," I can vividly remember what my initial reaction was.

First of all, it was visceral. I could feel the shock hit me and my wife. Then there was the sadness. Also, severe emotional disappointment struck, because I had wanted the most recent operation to be the last and to be able get back to the fantastic opportunity I had been given to live out my life. I had thought I was back to my goal to die with this cancer, not from it, and then, in a moment, I was back to being not so sure.

Some cancer patients talk of feeling anger; I imagine that is a valid emotion but one I never experienced. Who or what was I to be angry at?

What would anger do at that moment, other than distract me from finding a solution to this immense new dynamic in my life? Once the initial shock wore off, each time I found my self-talk wanting me to move on. As our kids might say when they hear someone whining, my self-talk was saying "Get a life!"

Ridding ourselves of anger is incredibly important to empowering our immune system rather than debilitating it.

So I did, each time. I started thinking of how I was going to deal with this monster disease I had embraced as part of my life. I wanted once again to prove I was the host, it was the guest, and I say when it leaves. Secondly, I wanted to determine how I acted and interacted with my friends and the outside world in general with my changed self. I knew I had the "partial evil" again; now I had to choose to continue to seek out the "universal good" that Pope continually reminds me exists in this world.

The Meteor

Back in 1986, with my first challenge and then the false alarm later that year, my perceptions changed as radically and suddenly as the arrival of the disease. Being told you have cancer is like being hit with a meteor from outer space that impacts your life and the lives of those around you. My focus before cancer with my first wife, Lori, was on lifelong goals like building retirement funds and raising our kids. With cancer, my focus changed to the very short term. Instead of seeing far in front of us and setting long-term goals, I began focusing on enjoying what time I had left.

At times, I just wanted to live in the moment and enjoy the experiences of each day. For another, I began noticing all of those little, previously insignificant things in life. I was now feeling life as I lived it rather than denying myself those experiences and feelings and pushing them off for future benefit. My feelings about all things, big or small, were much more acute. This is when one of the mottos I've mentioned came to be. It was simply, "keep on keepin' on! Each moment was exquisite, not without occasional severe pain, but always with immense pleasure.

Yes, I began thinking one step at a time, and I found these steps would be in a very different direction than I had ever considered before.

At forty-two years of age, I found that having cancer could induce a midlife crisis. As I began to realize I might survive, I thought of the things I wanted to do with my life. The answers inside my head were surprising and even shocking. Maybe I would survive, but would our twenty-year marriage? The eventual answer became a startling *no*.

We had both changed so much over twenty years and really hadn't calculated those changes into our relationship until that meteor hit us and showed us the cracks that had grown in that relationship. I found myself thinking about trying to be around for my daughter's high school graduation, but all the long-term goals Lori and I had seemed far-fetched, even ridiculous in light of the doctors' diagnosis. My self-talk back then was racing out in many new directions.

Shifting back to the present, one big step in self-talk I focused on in my most recent experience in 2010 was the act of forgiveness—for my own benefit. Yes, you read that right. The act of forgiveness is as much or more for me as it is for the person I'm forgiving. The "partial evil" of my cancer coming back for this fourth time had given me a "universal good" gift, that of understanding the worth of forgiveness.

Forgiveness

In my life, I have struggled with the effort of forgiveness. I have remained pretty angry with a few people who have lied to me or disappointed me or hurt me in an undeniable way. In 2010, I thought about it some more in the light that the chemotherapy was not working and we had not yet found surgeons willing to operate this time. Was I going to die feeling angry at those people? I realized, once again, I had a choice.

To me, forgiveness is another part of our life experience that has a twist when you try it. We all know people who have disappointed us, right? I'm no different in that. So in the exercise of putting myself in my best light in my own mind—being my own best friend—I thought of the people for whom I was carrying anger and other negative feelings.

Knowing that I might be looking at my last days, I wanted to live out my life with grace. How could I do that with the anger I was carrying? I began to read a piece about the act of forgiveness in a religious sense.

After that reading, eventually, I had a moment of clarity. Those whom I resented were not less comfortable because of my latent anger. I was. Talk about a "reset."

So I created a list of anybody for whom I felt negativity. Then I used my self-talk to forgive each name on the list. Once I did that, I spoke each name and said out loud, "I forgive you." That actually started to reset my feelings for those people.

They were the same people after I did this, but I was beginning to feel better and better.

I walked from the den to our bedroom with a smile and told my wife I was no longer angry at anybody. It was freeing to be able to tell Olivia that. Since then, I have had the opportunity in conversation with friends to mention my new status. They were discussing their anger with someone, and I found myself truthfully saying I had no ill will toward anybody anymore.

When I thought there was no surgical solution for what I faced and while under the effects of a devastating chemotherapeutic set of drugs, I had my proverbial back against the wall. I wanted to achieve this form of grace as I dealt with the possibilities that the chemotherapy might not be successful, and we might never find surgeons willing to operate on me. I was motivated by threats of my death. But even if I had not felt so motivated, discovery of this power of forgiveness, with my self-talk helping me to believe and then reset, would still have given me this new sense of freedom.

Perfection

Every time cancer came back, I reminded myself to be kind and positive. Sounds simple, but when you don't feel well, maybe not so easy. And of course, I kept reminding myself to "keep on keepin' on."

But if these were my last days, besides forgiveness, there was so much more to do. Even more than usual, I wanted every experience with friends and family to be fun and meaningful. Many of Olivia's and my clients in our financial planning practice were our friends as well, so we were blessed with seeing a large number of our friends frequently. I don't need to tell you, though, that every experience with our friends and family wasn't meaningful and wonderful.

In 2010, as I dealt with the fourth reoccurrence, I thought about this somewhat irrational desire for perfection in my relations with family and friends and the resulting mild disappointment when perfection was not our experience. And sure enough, a new perspective started to wash over me. Was I getting peeved at those parties with whom I interacted when things went less than perfectly? Was I disappointing myself? Obviously, I was causing these feelings, not my friends and family.

By having this desire to see everyone often and have everything go so well, was I setting myself up for disappointment? Was I actually acting out some of my negative self-talk? It was saying to me, "You may have very little time left! Get busy. Rush! And make sure every engagement is a great memory." That was my new self-talk, and upon reflection, I didn't like the lofty expectations.

We Are Not in a Rush

So, I loaded a "replacement" into my self-talk. I reset a new saying to repeat often: "We are not in a rush." I had wanted to soak up as much life as possible in case it really was going to run out this time. Who could blame me? I was reacting to what I thought I knew: not only that the clock was running, but that it was running out. I was acting like a quarterback directing a two-minute drill in a football game. Whoa. Suddenly I felt foolish. So I forgave myself for acting as I had been and started over with a new calmness invoked every time I caught that negative "rush for perfection." Instead, I thought, *We are not in a rush.*

And then I wasn't.

When we had a chance to travel to Europe after the successful 2010 operation, we employed the "we are not in a rush" self-talk phrase throughout our trip. It made a huge difference in our enjoyment. When we started to tense up about arrangements or catching a train, one or the other of us would say, "You know what, we're not in a rush. If we make it, we make it. If not, there's another train." We had the greatest time.

Lori's Gifts

One of the greatest gifts I have been given in my life has come from Lori, my first wife. Ours was not a rough, lawyer-loaded, flailing around, mad-at-each-other divorce. Ours was a slow-rolling dissipation. When we realized where we were and that divorce was inevitable, we used the services of a marriage counselor and then a mediator. Rather than fight through lawyers, we managed to keep talking, and while we didn't understand some things about each other, we sat in the mediator's office and found ways to come to agreements around the edges.

One afternoon, while we were in conversation, things began to heat up. I believe the main issue was money and asset values; I can't remember the exact items we were at odds about. At one point, the mediator said, "Well, why don't we just look at every item we can't agree on from the kids' perspective and do whatever seems best for them? That's the way we'll resolve it." Lori, being the wonderful and smart person she is, did not think about this proposal very long before saying, "That seems like a reasonably good template. Let's try it." We moved forward with the mediator, resolving issues with relatively little discomfort.

I tell you the moments and the process of our divorce to give you some perspective about the gift Lori gave me. Actually, I now believe it is two gifts. First, she found a way to forgive me for my part, the active part, in our falling out after our trials with my cancer. I talk about grace off and on in this book as being something I aspire to. Well, Lori achieved it in our relationship after our divorce. She has acted with perfect grace over the years since our breakup.

We still sometimes ask each other, "What would the kids like?" but that's usually for Christmas or birthdays now. We talk frequently about everything the kids are doing and what we ourselves are doing. Lori has continued to be as helpful and kind to me during my cancer challenges as she ever was. We include each other in our lives and in the kids' lives. Her kindness is astonishing. The other gift derives from her first gift. She has also allowed me to forgive myself by her grace. I could not forgive myself without her forgiveness.

Lori visiting us at lunch

Be a Friend

The power of forgiving ourselves is a remarkable part of managing our self-talk. Remember, a good friend is one who listens. And a good friend is one who never stays angry for long or puts you down when things do not go well. Be your own best friend, and learn to forgive yourself through your self-talk when something goes wrong. It works just as effectively as when your good friend says he is sorry for saying something or apologizes for hurting your feelings in some way. Your mind will accept it in the same way, and you can "keep on keepin' on" with a consistently better feeling about yourself.

CHAPTER 15

COMPLETE RATHER THAN COMPETE: PARTNERS

God only knows what I'd be without you.
>>—The Beach Boys, "God Only Knows"

All people have one thing in common: they are all different.

>>—Robert Zend

I don't want to get too deep into psychoanalysis here, but honestly, there is something else going on for me that partnering resolves, and I'd like to share it with you. Some of us who have lost loved ones early may find we will always have a hollow feeling from that loss. We carry scars.

I usually feel I have moved beyond the pain of those early losses of my parents and then my brother. But I also believe their loss created, at least in part, the need for me to partner with others. I might say the partial evil of their loss led me to find my way to the good in my life, much of which is the result of effectively partnering with others.

I believe at critical times in my life, from my experience with Casey onward, partnering reduced or eliminated some of my deep-down twin fears of failure and loneliness. Partners were and are a part of that courage I have relied upon to "keep on keepin' on" when my self-talk turns inward and becomes self-defeating.

Casey was a gift from my father to me, a gift he was unable to bestow personally because of his own grief. Sometimes we need to find a partner to help us through the night, and for me, she was that person. I hope that my father's gift in Casey and how that gift helped me will become my gift to you in helping you cope with cancer or other setbacks and that you will look for qualities in partners who can do the same things for you.

There is nothing as damaging and unnecessary as feeling sorry for yourself. Millicent Fenwick, a congresswoman during the 1970s and early '80s, once said, "Never feel self-pity, it is the most destructive emotion there is. How awful to get caught up in the terrible squirrel cage of self." If you do not respect and love yourself, how can you expect others to do so? Instead, it has been my choice to do something about what makes me feel that way. At the least, I try to talk about it with a trusted partner to get back on my normally positive path. In previous chapters of this book, you see my praise for business professor Peter Drucker's marvelous urging, "The best way to predict the future is to create it." Feeling stuck? Find a partner who can power forward with you. Reach out. Expect the best, and make it happen.

What common traits did I look for when searching for a partner? And what was the sixth sense that I used to learn quickly to trust them and convey that they could trust me? There are several common traits in others that qualify them as potential partners:

1. *A mutual and compatible need.* The other person has to want to partner in a business or personal way. Both of you should look at the relationship as helping each other to be complete rather than compete.
2. *A nurturing nature.* Avoid toxic relationships. Mean people need not apply. I refer you back to the chapter analyzing the difference between a skeptic and a cynic. Cynics need not apply either.
3. *Common sense.* There is nothing as discouraging as having to work with someone who goes off on irrational tangents not associated with helping each other achieve common goals. Complete rather than compete with the other person.

4. *Friendliness.* Effective partners must have a sense of humor and understand the concepts of positive self-talk and quick resets. Life is good.

5. *Comfort.* Count on yourself and your first intuition. This trait reminds me of the advice I mentioned my dad gave me about friendship: whether or not someone likes us can often be determined simply by asking ourselves whether we like them. If we like them, chances are they like us, too. We do this, if only to confirm they are right to like us.

So let's see how I used partnering and these traits in the business side of my life as well as dealing with my cancer.

Yes, I lost both of my parents very early, but other than loneliness those three years after my mother died and before stepmom Casey arrived, I don't think I've ever been really alone. Well, maybe early on during my short, four-year navy career. Even then, I wasn't alone for long.

That's because in my navy experience, as an inexperienced ensign, I ended up being paired with a very salty, knowledgeable E-9 master chief during my first tour of duty. I came onboard my ship fresh from the Officer Candidate School (OCS) factory floor. At the time, I may have been twenty-three, but I still was carded frequently when we went out to a restaurant or bar. I was slight in stature and had, undeniably, a baby face.

I had graduated from college in 1966 during the Vietnam War buildup/ draft and, as you may remember from earlier, went directly from college to the US Navy Officer Candidate School in Newport, Rhode Island. Ninety days later, I was somehow an officer. I had spent another three months in Newport going through US Navy Communications School. Then I was on my way to becoming a ship's communications officer. I would be onboard a ship headed across the Pacific to the combat zone in the Gulf of Tonkin and South China Sea off the coast of Vietnam. I would be responsible for approximately thirty men in the operations division on a ship of about 240 enlisted men and officers, and tens of millions of dollars of equipment.

And I was on my own.

It was a twenty-three-year-old's dream coming out of OCS to be assigned to some glorious aircraft carrier conducting air ops while underway or at least to a sleek, fast destroyer cutting through the deep blue sea at thirty knots. However, "all partial evil, universal good" was afoot: I was appointed to the grimy old WWII-era tanker-oiler, USS Neches, AO-47, which was then in dry dock at Hunter's Point, a less than desirable, somewhat shabby area of San Francisco.

I arrived at the dry dock and my ship late in the evening and was escorted onboard and directly to my quarters by the man I was to replace. Bill was a good guy. He had four years in the service and had just been promoted a second time in his career. He was two grades above me. He was on his way to another ship for his next assignment in a few days. Bill was sandy-haired, and though relatively young, he was taller and looked older than I did by more than the few years that actually separated us. He was dressed in a rumpled, dirty-from-a-long-day khaki uniform and scuffed-up, long-ago-polished brown shoes. He told me to get some rest and join him and his troops for quarters at 0800 hours the next morning.

Okay, I thought with shaky but positive self-talk, *this is a clunky, 30-plus-year-old WWII workhorse of a ship, but I can make this work.* I slept pretty well that night because the long travel day had been exhausting. I felt super-nervous when I awoke the next morning and hurriedly got dressed. I put on my brand-new, perfectly creased pants, my perfectly folded shirt, and my shoes that glowed perfectly from all the shining I had to do during my schooling. Then I popped on my perfectly blocked hat with the shiny brass eagle insignia to go up the ladder (stairs) to quarters, the gathering of the ship's crew.

As I left my stateroom and proceeded through the passageway, I immediately caught the acrid smell of JP-5 (jet fuel) and oil in the air. I reached the next level, which was an open deck where some oil-stained hoses were lying. Others were hanging from the rigging. The gear had taken my attention, but as my head came above deck, I also realized I was coming up right behind Bill.

He heard me arriving and said to the troops, "Oh, and here is your new division officer, Ensign Bantz." He stepped aside and revealed me to the troops for the first time. There was dead silence—and then everybody laughed. For a split second, I had no clue; then I looked at the tall, scruffy fellow next to me with the salty green brass on his belt and hat from years at sea and realized the stark comparison they were seeing.

The shiny little ensign they saw began laughing with them.

Oh, yes. I sure needed a partner in this new very close-quartered forum. And I did not to have to look too long. I was blessed to have as my right-hand man one of the nicest guys I've ever met. He was a master chief, the senior enlisted man in my division. As they say in the navy, he was squared away.

Chief Rich Gannon was a highly qualified professional in navy communications, from all the equipment in the radio shack to the Combat Information Center (CIC) to the flags on the signal deck. Here came the "universal good" of my situation for the next two years as counterpoint to my not being on the perfect ship.

He sped up my orientation in every area in a calm and direct way. Most importantly, though, he became the partner I needed to deal with a much tougher situation than understanding equipment. The men in my division ranged in age from eighteen to fifty-five. He knew all the men incredibly well. I don't mean in a friendly way, although he was very friendly. I mean he knew their tendencies both at work and play and kept me on top of things. He acted as a buffer for me until I began to catch on. Over the next two years on that ship, Chief Gannon saved my bacon many times, and we got a lot done together.

Cancer Partners

Years later, when cancer arrived in my life, I found that some other cancer patients and people on doctors' staffs were very helpful and could even be comforting. They were not unlike my chief helping me to adjust to the shock of a new aspect in my life. Friends and some of the nurses and administrative assistants in doctors' offices can be a major source of information and comfort, helping to ease our way into our new lives with cancer.

I saw them as people who knew their way around and could make my new cancer-challenged life easier, just as the chief did in my new life onboard ship. In my last two encounters with the disease, my wife and I learned to seek these people out to guide and comfort us. In a way, Olivia and I took the approach of partnering up with these wonderful people, even though it was their job. I am still in touch with several of them because of the bond that formed as we went through my cancer experience.

The Business Side

Knowing how and when to partner has made a large difference throughout my life, including during my business years. I remember the day in 1976 when a casual friend, Don, called my financial services office on Monday after I had seen him at a church coffee. He knew I was relatively new in the business of financial advice, but we had several great conversations about economics, and I think he was intrigued and wanted to feel me out about using my services. I felt confident to discuss things with him because I had just finished my MBA program and had joined a national financial firm in downtown San Diego.

How exciting his call to me was for me for three big reasons: 1) he would probably be a very big client; 2) I was brand-new in the business, so I had very few clients in the first place; and 3) he was simply a nice guy. And it turned out that these things were exactly what he liked about me. He knew I was conversant in subjects he felt were important to his investing style; he knew I had very few clients, so he could command my attention; and he liked me (just as my dad had said). I know this because he actually told me those things right up front. He was a smart guy in many unorthodox but pleasant ways.

On the phone, he said, "Dave, would you please research several municipal bonds for me?" Municipal bonds are income vehicles popular with wealthy people because the interest they pay investors is tax-free. My self-talk was saying, "Uh-oh!" I knew all about economics and the stock market, but not much about munis, as they are known. Of course I said yes anyway, deciding I'd be staying really late at the office that night trying to play catch-up.

Munis are a market unto themselves. Each bond is different from the next, and remember, back in 1976, you couldn't turn to your computer and begin researching. There was no Bloomberg. There was no Google. There was very little public information on munis that could be obtained then without lots of digging. It took advisors years to become proficient at picking them. I knew I was on shaky ground. I needed to find someone in the office to shore up my obvious weakness.

The minute I was off the phone, I decided to look for Rich Zielony, one of the nicer guys in the office who I was pretty sure was purely a municipal-bond broker. I asked him a few questions and quickly confirmed I was in deep water. I had agreed to perform a service I really was not qualified to offer. I'd be making tracks to Rich's office every time Don called. As we talked, I felt we liked each other. I saw more to be gained by letting Don know I would be drawing on Rich's expertise than by trying to keep my ego intact as well as trying to keep all the business.

After a few more minutes of conversation, I knew I soon would be saying to Rich, "Is there a way we could work together longer term?" But for now, I said, "Rich, I'm not embarrassed to admit my naïveté to my client, and I think I'd rather keep the business and share with you than lose it all making some costly errors along the way." He smiled and responded by saying that he would be glad to pitch in on my immediate challenge.

Things went perfectly. I briefed Rich on everything I could think of regarding Don's finances and risk profile. He then researched the current bond inventory, checked market conditions, and reported back to me. This worked so well that Don was really pleased. He appreciated my being honest and involving an expert rather than trying to do the work by myself.

Don encouraged me to check with Rich in the future, saying, "You know whether you can work with him or not, David, but it seems to me you two did a pretty good job here. Think about it and talk with him." And I did. To be sure of my own desire to partner with him, I tried to think it through first. Don's push in the back was important, but I wanted to be settled in my own mind before asking Rich.

True to form, Rich answered me in a unique way, saying, "You know, I don't know much about stocks. Would you be able to help me with some of my bond clients who ask me about stocks?" Wow, a perfect solution was unfolding for both of us. We went on to work in a casual partnership for several years for a number of other clients. It benefited not only him and me but also our clients, as they received the best, most qualified advice from us in our specialties.

Looking at the common traits I mentioned earlier, Rich met all five:

1. *A mutual and compatible need.* Both of us looked at the relationship as helping each other to be complete rather than compete. He revealed he had a need as well as I did to partner. I became his "stock guy."

2. *A nurturing nature.* Rich was a really cheerful guy. He was a pleasure to be around. He took me under his "municipal wing" without making me feel foolish.

3. *Common sense.* This was an obvious and major attribute of Rich's personality. He was very analytical.

4. *Friendliness.* Rich had a great sense of humor and believed life is good.

5. *Comfort.* I counted on myself and my first intuition, as my dad had instructed me to when discussing friends. It works in business, too. We liked each other right away.

While this was the first time I sought a partnership to conquer a challenge in my business life (beyond the navy), as you know by now, it was not my first search for such an ally. Some people are loners, but my tendency through the years has been to choose to partner up when making big life steps. It is clear to me it started with Casey (remember our "pact" on the front steps?) and became a healthy pattern throughout my life.

There has always been an aspect of My Chi in my approach to partnering. The more I was able to "vacate myself" during and at the end of tasks by giving others credit—playing down my involvement in something we did together, even if I felt that I did 90 percent of it—the more I found I was "surrendering" to a higher ground of strength. This is another unexpected aspect of my people-management skills with My Chi. People usually knew what I had done without an announcement by me, so keeping my ego in check turned out to be worth it. This version of selflessness, while at times hard to execute, created positive energy, trust, and loyalty in my partnerships.

As I think about it, I am stunned at the number of times I have chosen to partner. There are many other examples, and they are not all work related. Some lasted only a short time and others for many, many years.

They even include the way I related to girlfriends. We look for mates for obvious reasons (don't laugh!), but beyond that dynamic, I have mostly tended to see my girlfriends as equal partners rather than attempt to control the relationship. There was always the My Chi of those relationships where, if I did have some control, it was the result of stepping aside and allowing my girl to come along with me on things we did rather than confronting and pushing her. Therefore, I sensed there was a lot of friendship involved in my versions of love life. And now, with my soul mate Olivia, there still is.

My first serious college girlfriend was a genius at math. I was, at that time, having a terrible time with the subject. She became not only the fun and lovely girl by my side at parties and football games; she also became my partner in the form of an occasional tutor as I tried to get my homework done and have a better understanding of what I was studying. We both appreciated the different facets of our relationship.

I wish I could tell you I paid rapt attention to her tutoring; however, she had other facets I paid attention to that shortened a number of those sessions. (I said don't laugh.) Of course, I'm not the only one who sees his/her love life as a partnership. It strikes me that some of the best and strongest relationships we come upon in life are those where the couple would speak of each other as best friends. After all, best friends are partners we can count on in good times and in bad.

Doubly Rich

I continued using the same partnership format I used with Chief Rich Gannon and my office mate Rich Zielony throughout the rest of my business career. It is obvious to me as I look back that this partnership-in-business strategy enabled me to get a great start in the navy and then a solid start in my business, which led to building a thirty-three-year financial planning career with five other successive partners through those years.

When one partnership came to a natural end, as happened with Rich (I left that office for another in our third year, and he moved to Oregon), I always seemed to find another mutually useful arrangement with someone else. I had learned a great deal from Rich about municipal bonds and felt I was now able to conduct my municipal business on my own thanks to his efforts. It had been a wonderful experience partnering with him. However, times changed; now it seemed just as natural for me to use partnering to find someone who was very knowledgeable about the evolving importance of retirement plans.

Business Partners Plus

Many of my clients needed to use retirement plans to meet their personal financial goals. Congress had passed a series of laws creating a group of tax-advantaged savings vehicles during the 1970s. Huge growth was now occurring in these plans, aimed primarily at the baby boomers moving up through the work force. This was a complicated and legalistic area of the investments business. Realizing by now that working with a partner was clearly my most comfortable way to manage and grow my business, I again began looking around my office. But no one seemed to have the expertise I knew I would need to go confidently to companies in San Diego and offer retirement plans to them and their employees.

Then one day, I realized I was in a bind. A friend had referred his one hundred-or-so employee company to me as my first sizable 401(k) retirement plan client. With a great opportunity and no way to responsibly go after the business, I thought back to the firm I had been with a few years previously. Sure enough, I remembered a lady there who had served as the director of marketing and also knew a great deal about retirement plans.

Her name was Olivia, and yes, you may recognize her name, because she eventually became my wife. At the time, however, my interest in her was that she knew a great deal about retirement plans. I called her and said, "Olivia, I have a great opportunity to make a 401(k) plan proposal to a private company here in San Diego. Would you be able to come over to my office after your workday and take a look at my proposal? Unfortunately, I've waited until the last moment. My meeting is at the end of this week."

It was my good fortune that she said yes, because we ended up working together to build a client base of more than thirty plans for small- to medium-sized companies in addition to the business I had created over the years advising individuals and families. We joked that she would "leave work to go to work" because we were so successful in putting these bids together. Actually, she put them together. My part of the partnership was to find the opportunities and then present her well-constructed proposals to the new clients.

This was a perfect blend of skills. After awhile, another partnership joke emerged. We said that I would go out and make promises to put a company's plan together, come back and tell her what I had promised—and then she would sit down and try to make me an honest man by finding a way to keep those promises.

Hiring My Partner

By the end of our first year doing this, I was talking with the resident manager of my office about hiring Olivia away from her employer to work solely with us.

I used my best My Chi as I considered his needs as well as mine. He likely would challenge me by saying that hiring her was too expensive. I prepared myself. I listened and engaged the manager, negotiating with him rather than directly arguing with him (blocking his punch and "fighting" with him) about the expense. I surrendered to his point. I agreed with his point that hiring her would be an increased cost, thereby neutralizing his argument. I surrendered, only to take control by suggesting she could be a resource not just to me, but also to others in the office. That way, she would enable far more revenue than needed to cover her expense. She would then be a revenue generator for the whole office. The My Chi move prevailed, he agreed, and fortunately, that was what transpired.

Of all the business partnerships, both before my arrangement with Olivia and after (we hired more partners to join us once our own partnership was firmly established), only one of them was antagonistic in its conclusion. However, all partial evil, universal good: our next partner, Derryck Jones, became involved with us as an immediate remedy to the problems the antagonistic partner had created. Derryck ended up being the best of all of our business partners. You may remember from a previous chapter that he bought our business when Olivia and I retired. Now that's a successful conclusion to a successful partnership. By the way, I am thrilled to say Derryck's business is thriving.

How did I find my partners? It might seem to be happenstance, but it wasn't. I would try to clearly identify why I wanted and needed to partner and list the reasons in my head. Think of my five common traits of a good partner. Now think back to my description of forming that first loose partnership with Rich. In that situation, I had a very identifiable need.

I found a person who filled that need short term first and foremost, to achieve my immediate objective.

But, in the back of my mind, I began to realize as I talked with Rich and Don, I had a larger, longer-term need that could be served by our arrangement and began evaluating Rich without offering anything immediately. It was serendipity in Rich's and my case that he needed to fill a gap in his services to his clients as well. But in truth, it took working with Rich to prepare for Don to see that we had the right skills and personalities to match each other in the categories of my five traits.

That blend of personality and skills, listed in the five common traits of a potentially great partner, had to be functional not only between the two of us. It also had to work for my clients and Rich's clients, should there be a need for interpersonal cross-contact. I wanted to be sure my clients could get along with him if they had to meet and vice versa.

The same can be said for the way in which I chose Olivia. I had a clear short-term need—to create a sophisticated retirement proposal. She was by far my best choice in terms of qualifications. How well we would work together, I wasn't sure, but I had worked well with her on much smaller tasks at the firm where we first met. After that and our first retirement plan experience, we both had the data and experience to evaluate what the longer term prospects were. They were so great, we decided to partner forever.

I mentioned positive self-talk as one of the common traits of a good partner. Self-talk can turn quite negative with the rejection involved in many business settings, especially those where the sales process is involved. The financial advisory business had then and still has one of the highest rates of individual failure in the first two years of any business.

Beyond the increased professionalism, partnering with Rich or Derryck or Olivia automatically gave me someone to talk with and consult with when times became tough.

Also, even though I might have been considered the affable sales and marketing kind of guy of most groups I formed, the capability and personality differences of my partners attracted clients I myself would never have attracted. More importantly, I can think of many of our clients we would not have kept except for our differences. To the surprise and delight of our clients, we often displayed these differences openly in client meetings as a positive part of our team. The breadth of skills, opinions, knowledge, and experiences provided our clients with far more than any one of us could hope to provide.

Nice Guys Finish First with Medical Partners

From my business experiences, you have seen partnering as a way of conquering new and untried ways of doing business, attracting new/ different clients, or rapidly gaining the knowledge to offer unfamiliar products or services in a business setting. Now imagine how a cancer patient like me was able to transfer this format to partnering with doctors, nurses, and even my relatives to overcome the many obstacles that a cancer challenge presents. Wouldn't you like to work with a doctor who wants to help you get well, has a compatible need, has common sense, has a good "bedside manner," and to whom you can tell your true feelings and condition?

This process is similar to what Olivia and I did as we "partnered" with the nurses and doctors' assistants in the medical community to deal with my cancer the last two times it returned. We didn't consider them as voices on the other end of the phone to set appointments. We really teamed up with them and involved them in our lives. We were not afraid to ask them hundreds of questions. We tried to demonstrate great and genuine appreciation for each person's efforts. We acted in a way that let them know they were our partners, too; we hoped they felt what we knew to be true, that they had a stake in my treatment.

The day after my most recent surgery in 2010, the lead doctor, Dr. Andrew Lowy, came by the ICU, where I was to be generally unconscious for six days, to check in on my recovery. I had had a bad night and had to be put in restraints, meaning they had had to strap me down because I was acting violently in my drug-induced coma. Obviously I didn't hear them, but Olivia later told me the conversation between her and the doctor went something like this: Olivia, apologetically and with a bit of wonder, said to the doctor, "I don't know why he's doing this, doctor; he is never, ever violent at home. He's just such a nice guy." Dr. Lowy comforted my wife with kind words, saying, "I know. That's part of why we operated on him." They were my partners—both of them.

Opposites Attract—And Get Things Done

Another thing I observed in forming my series of partnerships is that opposites attract—and they work and play well together. As you now know, my lasting partnership with Olivia started first in business and then over years progressed to marriage, and then, thankfully, to multiple successful efforts in surviving cancer. Our partnership works because she had, and still has, an entirely different skill set than I do. She can soak up an incredible amount of information and quickly organize it in a cogent, understandable form. As you can imagine, this was a valuable trait when dealing with the medical community. However, in our working years, she was less comfortable with finding the client and offering the proposal. That is where I could close the deal.

Rarely has it been a volatile office environment or marriage/ lifestyle, because we both realize how much we benefit from our differences. It might seem more comfortable to find someone like yourself who likes the same things and does the same things, which we generally do. But I think this is another part of life that is surprising. I don't mean this as an absolute, but I firmly believe looking for opposites, that is complements, in my partnerships has given me more success and a more complete life experience.

While Olivia and I do have things in common, like enjoying skiing, golf, friends, wines, and travel, we are definitely not alike. Just ask her. It might seem overly dramatic, but I'll let you decide: Olivia has saved my life several times in several ways. She has used her remarkable skill set on my behalf not only at work, and not only to handle lots of details in our personal lives that I might miss, but also when life and death have been involved. The obvious times I mention here are different from and in addition to her courageous stands with me as we faced cancer challenges again and again.

I cannot tell you the myriad times Olivia has stepped up either emotionally or in many other meaningful ways, such as continually breaking down the code of our health care system during all of my cancer adventures. The author of an article about my case in *Cancer Care*, published by UCSD's Moores Cancer Center in the summer of 2013, identified her value by saying she has been my "fiercest advocate" through these critical times.

Nine Lives

What are those times other than when dealing with cancer? Here we go. A few years back, before we had won our last run-in with cancer, I came limping across the house to where she was in the bedroom. I said something like, "Rrivia, I thin sumthhin is wroon. I can'tyyyyype anymo." She took one look at me and knew by my drooping lips, numbness in my left arm, and lack of balance that I was having a stroke. She raced me out of the house to a hospital in San Diego, an hour and fifteen minutes away from our mountain home. She somehow made it in time for the docs to diagnose proper treatment in the emergency room. Within a couple of days, I was released from the hospital seemingly no worse for the wear. Now that's a quick-thinking partner.

Or how about this one? May of 2012, we were traveling through the country and spent several days visiting Arches National Park on the edge of Moab, Utah. It was beautiful, and we were walking everywhere. We noted how windy it was several times during the three days we were there. I thought the flying dust was the reason I had to blow my nose so much. So I kept blowing and blowing, harder and harder, thinking somehow, it would come to an end. But it didn't, at least not in the way I thought it would.

The last day, we went back up into the park and found the last remarkable sandy brown arch we wanted to see before leaving. I was stuffier than ever. As we pulled into the parking lot, I looked at Olivia and said, "You know, I think I've seen enough arches that I can miss this one. I have a headache, and I think I'll just wait for you here in the car." She asked if I was really all right, because I am so active that this was totally out of character. I said again, "Yes, really, I'll be fine here." So she left to get her last couple of pictures.

When she returned to the car about ten minutes later, I was curled up in a ball on the passenger's seat somewhat delirious from the agony that had developed during the mere few minutes she was away. I was wracked with excruciating pain in my head. She stood outside the car with her back to my window for a minute to take another picture and I couldn't even bring myself to tap on the window, let alone open the door. When she opened the driver's side door, she immediately knew we were into another weird medical emergency.

The 911 operator told her it would be faster for her to drive the ten miles out of the park rather than for paramedics to find us, so she got behind the wheel and focused on finding her way to a small medical center just outside that entrance to the park. They semi-carried me in to the MRI room of their facility and rapidly deduced I was having some kind of brain hemorrhage. It was a subdural hematoma, which means the hemorrhage was on the outside of my brain and the blood was rapidly flooding into the space between my brain and my skull. The more it flooded, the more pressure it put on the nerves in my brain. Not good for the brain, and *ouch!* Major pain.

Olivia gave the staff a printed copy of my (long) medical history, which she always carries with her. It is chronological (you saw it in the front of this book). That history and the results of the scan persuaded them to helicopter me from Moab, Utah, to a major regional hospital in Grand Junction, Colorado. This hospital had the physical plant and staff to care for my kind of emergency. I was flown by helicopter, and Olivia had to drive the two hours to join me. Today, when Olivia tells the story, she points out that I had a helicopter flight over some of the most spectacular scenery in the United States. The only problem was that I was only half-conscious and lying face up.

Three days later, kind Doctor Robert Fox, who was tending to me, said the flow seemed to have stopped and the amount of blood had stabilized. They would not need to operate, at least not at this time. I could go home, but I was not to bend over for any reason for the next month. They thought if I remained quite inactive, the blood would have a good chance of draining without surgery. Olivia had done it again. I'm guessing she wasn't thrilled with who would be doing all the bending and lifting for the next month, but because of her smarts, cool response, and persuasiveness, I was on my feet showing my back to yet another hospital.

The postscript: about three weeks later, one evening around seven, we were home after having had a check-up MRI to see what developments were occurring with my simultaneously diagnosed nasal polyps, which were the real reason for my stuffy nose in the park. We received a phone call from the hospital radiologist. Olivia picked up and I heard her say, "Really? A problem? Okay. How early do we need to be there tomorrow? You know we live an hour and a half out of the city. Oh, tonight? Really? Oh my gosh. Okay, we're leaving right now."

Good grief, I thought. Here we go again. They operated that night. I now can reach up and feel two fingertip-sized indentations remaining from the two holes they drilled into the high right side of my gray head that night to relieve the pressure that was again beginning to build. It had built up enough that the blood shot out when the docs drill broke through. Just in time. She did it yet again. That's my partner.

I admit that, being the active and sometimes impatient guy that I am, I probably had pushed the limits of recovery from a subdural hematoma by walking up and down my steep driveway. Mea culpa.

Olivia and I had come to know each other so well as we worked together that it was obvious to me she was a wonderful woman, a true partner, whom I could count on time and again. Through these years, as circumstances widened, that same trust has remained between us. Little did she or I know what that was to mean or the depths to which our mutual trust would be tested.

Many times, each one of us had the other to help clear the way to move on to success or just to keep on keepin' on. And that's what most all of us want in the end: a successful career and also a successful experience with someone we love. If you find a partner different from yourself in constructive ways and you can learn to consistently trust and nurture each other, magic happens daily.

CHAPTER 16

HOW GOES THE BATTLE?

They shook hands affectionately, and Lord Nelson said: "Well, Hardy, how goes the battle? How goes the day with us?-"

"Very well, my Lord," replied Hardy.

—Lord Nelson hearing of his success in the historic sea Battle of Trafalgar just before he died in 1805. From "The Death of Lord Nelson" (1807), William Beatty

After the first cancer attack, my whole life view changed dramatically. It was as if I had no choice in the matter. My mind shifted to temporary auto-pilot after that huge operation. First wife Lori and I had had all sorts of long-view life goals during our twenty years together. Then, in a moment, they shifted to the background in my mind. It was an abrupt and disturbing change, but as you know, we've adjusted over the years to the change. We're very good friends to this day.

We recently had dinner together and, as we looked back, she and I agreed, "Those goals, wonderful on the surface, insidiously took over our lives." When my cancer struck at age forty-two, we suddenly began realizing we were not enjoying each day and had not been for a while. We had allowed many pressures from work, children, home building and remodels, our individual commitments to church and nonprofit boards in the community, and other activities to take over just as so many young couples do. In other words, without our realizing it, we had subtly made our relationship vulnerable to sudden shock. We were not doing the things together as a couple that might alert us to this growing weakness.

Then cancer hammered home the reality of our mortality. It hadn't been there. Now it was there. My priorities were irreversibly shuffled. There was nothing subtle about it. Suddenly, my mind's eye shifted from the faraway financial and other long-term goals that had been like beautiful mountains on the far horizon for us if we had been on a hike, the promised land of retirement, and the good life after working so hard. We didn't know it, but we were out of balance.

Lori and I were relentlessly pursuing those long-term goals at the expense of our current life pace and happiness—and apparently, my health. We were thinking it was just a matter of time. But now, maybe those idyllic goals were a mirage; they were no longer there and now certainly not within my predicted lifespan. I became aware that focusing on those long-term goals came at the expense of enjoying each day. Rather than the mountains in the distance, I began looking no further than the next bed of flowers along the sidewalk, so to speak, for joy and satisfaction. The balance in our lives shifted violently, and everything changed. The major casualty was our twenty-year marriage.

Getting Cocky

Over the years, I endured those four major cancer surgeries. After each occurrence, I was alive and getting healthy again. The partial evil of the returning cancer and subsequent surgeries, with patience, kept evolving to the universal good of survival. Physically, I continued to find a way to be resilient, and I was still thriving in terms of maintaining a wonderful "normal" lifestyle. Within six months of each occurrence, in spite of missing major organs and significant portions of my core muscle structure, I was back to playing tennis, snow skiing, golfing, going on frequent walks and runs, and doing a lot of traveling. But then, as you know by now, the year 2010 held something unimaginable even for this cancer-toughened guy.

Looking back, I think I had gotten cocky after my successful third surgery at M. D. Anderson in 1998. I had gone past the five-year requirement for cancer checks by MRI or CT scan. I even was able to get some new life insurance. I really thought that huge challenge and my conquest of that 1998 surgery would be the grand finale of my cancer experience. Life had become so normal again after my kidney-plus removal. But now I see that with that mindset, I had put myself back at risk. I should have remained vigilant.

Try putting yourself in my shoes at this moment. Imagine being told for the fifth time, "You have a little more than a year to live." Your cancer has returned and, this time, spread vertically through your abdomen and into your chest and is as massive as the first episode. Fear began to well up as I self-talked—self-lectured, really—that this was happening because I became careless. I failed to realize it had reoccurred and had been growing for years. I felt at fault. My self-talk was criminalizing me. This was a new emotion in my journey. Doctors told me it was more widespread than ever before and, yes, it was the same dreaded cancer I have vowed to "live with rather than die from." Again? Oh, no. Not again! Really? Ah, denial.

Thanks, but No Thanks

Another deadly challenge. And then it got tougher. As you know from a previous chapter where I talked about feeling like I was locked in a white room, several surgeons, even the one who successfully had done what doctors called a heroic operation removing my right kidney and surrounding area eleven years earlier, said they thought surgery was too complicated and risky and would not operate this time. First of all, risk of surgery for whom, them or me? On top of "no surgical solution," they told me they could only provide me with chemotherapy and palliative care. How would you feel if this were you?

These, then, were the facts of my new reality in early 2010 right after retirement. Happy New Year, Dave. One month into retirement from a career of thirty-three years, was it going to be my fate to die in 2010 of inoperable cancer after all? I tried to stay calm and made myself ask: *What should my reaction be?* I knew I must keep predicting my future by creating it to incorporate my Drucker phrase. *But how do I do that with this real threat?*

My immediate emotional response—my unbridled self-talk, if you will—said, "Now chemo, well okay. But my interpretation of palliative care is that it is a way of saying you are going to die but we may be able to help you live a little longer and make your death a little less painful." Thanks, but no thanks. I wasn't resigned to that—yet.

I tried to calm my self-talk because, yes, I had heard this speech several times over the past twenty-five years. But even though my resolve was shaken, I thought to myself, *Thanks, but no thanks. It has been my choice each time to choose high-risk surgery to try to live a longer life, and so far, so good.* My subconscious response was, perhaps more importantly, *If they're right and I'm wrong, what do I do with my short time left?* Now tell me, what's the point of fighting cancer while accepting palliative care, in my case, other than to live a little longer and therefore be blessed with the time to say my good-byes while my organs get beaten to a pulp with chemo and then fail? Then I die gracefully? I don't think so. I knew I had to rededicate myself to efforts to find a surgeon who would (co)operate. I was the host and cancer the visitor. I needed to show it the door by surgery, and if I died on the table, maybe that was better than the slow version of death I was facing.

Let's think about this "no thanks" response to palliative care and fighting. Palliative care has some marvelous uses. Recently, it has been employed when a patient has multiple ailments. If a person has breast cancer and stomach cancer, it can be the method that sustains her between the two separate procedures as she regains her strength. But in my case, it was only being offered as a slight life-extender and as a pain-management system as I died. That was not my wish. I still believed there was a way to live with this cancer, to die with it not from it.

For some of us, fighting may be the most comforting way to think about dealing with cancer. It is a relatively automatic and instinctive emotional response we spoke of in a previous chapter to any threat or invasion of our happiness, our status quo. It allows us to strike out at things and to be righteously angry. That might feel good, but is that the best thing for us?

No Fighting Allowed

So "how goes the battle?" I have always been turned off by politicians who use the phrase "I will fight for you." Why are they fighting for me? I want them working with others to get/keep needed government services in place and remove the others that are abuses of our system, not fight with each other. So it is with my cancer. Personally, I am not comfortable with the vision of fighting with my cancer. I knew I was not about to believe the doctors and give up after all I had been through. I had to keep thinking rather than emotionally fighting with no clarity. I found my self-talk dialogue doggedly looking for another way to think about my new and greatest challenge.

To envision fighting can be an empowering reaction for some people, enabling them to battle back from misadventures of any kind. This is especially true when dealing with a cancer that roars into their lives, unexpected and large. I know that's how I responded to my first encounter, as that was the phrase everyone used, from my friends and relatives to the doctors: "We're gonna fight this with you, Dave!" Some oncologists teach their patients to literally envision their cancer cells and picture smashing them to bits, one by one.

Again, it may be enabling for some, but it could be a denial strategy, and if their fight is unsuccessful, tremendous discouragement and sadness may be all that is left as time dwindles for both the patient and survivors. How do you feel when your favorite team or player loses in a sport? Right, you feel let down, low, and irritated, even sad. Imagine yourself and your loved ones realizing in the last days, you are losing your "fight" for your life.

Importantly, I do not want to take anything away from those of us who are choosing to deal with cancer or other problems in this way. My concern is it may be short-term pleasurable in the same way it was (wrongly) pleasurable for me to explode with anger, as I had done with granddaughter Lucy. I believe I have found a way that makes me more able to deal a death blow to my cancer while living out my life, however long, with grace rather than anger.

The Better Way

There is a better way—at least, it is for me. Fortunately or unfortunately, depending on how you look at it, I've had more than a few chances to try different approaches, and I think I have found a better one than fighting.

What is that better choice? You know I chose my mental version of the ancient art of fighting: t'ai chi, or for me, My Chi. I chose to use this idea to embrace my cancer, to invite my cancer into my life and own it. I chose to live with the cancer rather than block and resist and struggle with it. I did not and do not now deny my cancer's existence or even its effects on me. Make no mistake; my will to live is not affected by this way of thought. It is just that embracing and living with my cancer and managing it, however long, without the stress and concurrent anger and fear of fighting it appeals to me. With this approach, it matters not to me whether I am cancer-free or it is still with me. I now will be ever watchful for its possible recurrence, but I have conquered it and made it a normal part of my life. Knowing this, I can live with peace and calm.

This way of thinking blends with another realization: whether I am right and the doctors and naysayers are wrong, or vice versa, I want to live the rest of my life with grace. It may seem paramount to know whether I am right and I can eradicate the cancer and go on to live a long life, or I am wrong and have only a few months to live—but as I've thought about this, I realized it is not. The length of my life is secondary. What am I going to do with the time, and how will I live in that time? That is my paramount focus.

If I have only a short time left on this earth, why use it fighting? I have realized that question is also valid for the long term.

Let God choose my time here. I should be answering my question, "What's the point?" In other words, what do I want to do with the time I have left, whatever the length of time might be? So it has become my challenge to myself to live my life with bright optimism based on faith and determination without regard to the time left. I cannot control the time. I *can* control my self-talk and actions.

Whatever You Say

With that realization, I began to learn how to embrace my cancer and accept its existence for the present. I adjusted my "self-talk and reset" method to be mindful of embracing, not fighting. I also chose to adjust my life and expectations for the future to be as happy as I could while enduring the experience. I tried to be open and matter-of-fact with my friends and colleagues about my cancer so they, too, could accept it as a part of me.

I began to live a version of my former and ongoing life that was pleasing to me and especially to Olivia. One time during the four months of chemo in 2010, when I was being a bit argumentative with Olivia, I just wore out when we determined she was right, which meant I was wrong—again—about whatever we were discussing. I looked over at her, smiled weakly, and with a bit of My Chi, said, "You know what, dear? No more battles. I'm going to make it easier for both of us. From now on, I'm just going to do whatever you say. Then we'll both be happier." I did just that for the remaining months of chemo, and it was marvelous for both of us.

It is now a running joke. Sometimes she says, "I'd agree with you, Dave, but then we'd both be wrong." Or when we get a bit wound up about something, with a wry smile, she'll say, "Why can't you be like you were when you were taking chemo?" Don't tell her this, but I think she's right—again.

As I was enduring the drastic effects of that chemotherapy in 2010 (you may remember, I dropped from 160 pounds to 125 pounds and went bald rapidly), Olivia and I said, "Enough!" We decided to call her cousin and his wife, favorite travel companions of ours, and invite them to go with us to Alaska. Voila! We couldn't hike or take a rugged drive through Denali National Park, but we could take a cruise up the Inland Passage. That way, I could enjoy the views from the ship while underway and rest in our ship's cabin whenever I ran out of steam. They would have many things to do, including taking some of the side trips when in port while I napped onboard. I could sit with them at dinner and share the day's events, even if I didn't eat much—okay, anything.

What a great way it was for "Baldy" (that was my nickname by that time) and everyone else to feel better and not be moping around waiting for the next doctor's appointment. I was living with my cancer by embracing it and enjoying the time I had. *Optimism, faith,* and *determination* were my self-talk repeat words whenever I started to slip off into negativity and despair. We all had a great time.

Cousin Peyton with us in Alaska

Grateful and Graceful

There is an important number in our lives: 86,400. That is the number of seconds we have each day. And we can't save those seconds for the future. They are gone forever. If we don't use those seconds well today, when we go to bed tonight, they are lost. Some have equated it to a bank account with a daily deposit of $86,400 that goes away at the end of each day if we don't spend it. Many of us cancer survivors know every second counts. The threat of losing time has taught us its preciousness. This doesn't mean we run around being more productive. It means we must find a way to be happy, to enable and allow others around us to be happy, to love deeply, and to enjoy life. When we allow ourselves to think this way, priorities subtly or even overtly change. You might even say we become more grateful and graceful.

There is a comfortable urgency (how about that for an oxymoron) about each day that I don't remember feeling before my cancer. I took many things for granted. After living many years on the coast, we now live in San Diego's backcountry at 3,200 feet in the mountains. When I look out my den window and see the sun dropping in the west, I call out "Sunset!" to Olivia when it is particularly beautiful, which is almost every day. She knows what that means. We try to share every sunset together. Sometimes, when she hears me call out, she pours glasses of celebratory wine to sip as we watch the end-of-day beauty unfold. It's a lovely way to spend some of those precious seconds. Every day now is a gift I did not expect to have at times in my life.

Here's a bit of good news for you. You don't need to contract cancer to do this. Major reset. Start self-talking "86,400," and adjust your priorities to respect that number. Cheers. Enjoy life starting now. It is never too late.

Warner Springs Sunset

CHAPTER 17

BE A CONQUEROR

The mind, once stretched out by an empowering idea, can
never fully shrink to its original dimensions.
—Oliver Wendell Holmes, paraphrased

Have you done your one courageous act for today? We should all go to bed every night with the mindset that we have done at least one courageous act for ourselves or someone else during the day.

As you no doubt have noticed by now, I am an avid collector and user of aphorisms. It's part of my attitude-reset strategy to get back on track quickly and get on with the best parts of my life. Mark Twain had a wonderful aphorism I have used to reset my self-talk and attitude many times. It reads: "Do that thing you fear most, and the death of fear is certain." That requires a courageous act.

I think back to childhood actions that prove this thought in small ways time after time. I became a gymnast as a school kid. Unbeknownst to me when I was about seven, my mom began dealing with what would be four years of worsening cancer. As I've noted, she died when I was eleven. I say "unbeknownst," but you know kids have a sixth sense about these things, and I just knew something was wrong with my mom.

During these years, I became close to anorexic, maybe in part because of my mother's illness. But where there is bad, look for the good. Because I was small, I could run like the wind, effortlessly throw my body around, and do gymnastics basics like cartwheels and somersaults. I remember the moment when that play became an attempt to become a real gymnast. I also remember the fear attached to the moment.

As you may remember from an earlier chapter, my older brother, Bob, in his teen years was a great and classic big brother. Even though he was seven years older than I was, he played with me a lot. He was a fantastic athlete in general, but specifically, he was a basketball star in high school. I can still picture the local Schenectady newspaper sports page headline one morning: "Bantz scores 33, school record." There was a center page above-the-fold picture of him taking a jump shot. There is no doubt that I idolized him then.

One weekend when we were playing in the front yard, Bob thought it would be great if I had a new-and-improved way to get to my school bus each morning. Instead of walking down the driveway, I was to run across our small upper lawn from our front door, jump off the two-foot-high stone wall, do a front flip to the lower lawn, land in stride, and run on to the bus stop with all the kids watching from the bus.

What?

Well, I liked the attention from my brother, and it sounded kind of cool, but, yeow, jumping off a wall and doing a flip? I wasn't keen on the idea. Oh well, if I could just do it the first time. Yes, do that thing you fear to do, and the death of that fear is certain.

By the end of the morning, my brother had convinced me I could do a front flip off the wall. Forget about the facts we thought of later: *I'll be carrying books; I'll have a heavy coat on in upstate New York during September when school starts,* etc. No matter, I finally actually did it. As I think back on it, I did it mostly because I believed in my brother beyond the fear I felt. In a way, he was my "feather." Then afterward, the fear disappeared.

The point of this story is the first time I did it, I crashed down on my tail with a three-quarter flip. Ouch! But hey, I was okay. My brother cheered. The fear was gone. I was right back up on top of the wall. I did it over and over until I could easily land on my feet and keep running.

No, I never did it on the way to my school bus, but I went on to do a running flip in gym class for the gym teacher. He then put me on a trampoline for the first time, and I was hooked. Seat drops became back drops, front drops, then back flips, front flips with half-twists, full twists, turntables, and I was off and running. Talk about the death of a fear. I kept at it and went on to win All-Around Gymnast of the Year my senior year in high school. Still have the trophy. I even taught trampoline my freshman year in college to earn a few bucks.

I Own You!

I can't remember when or where, but I know age played a role in my starting to lose that mindset. I woke up one morning and realized I had let fear creep into parts of my adult life. I was genuinely fearful of making a business presentation later that day. As young adults and then adults, a different perception of risk moves insidiously into many areas of our lives.

As I thought about this development, I believed I could convert the thought process of conquering my youthful fear of physical risk to the challenges of those days in business. It could be a path for overcoming fear in general, but I was wrong. That was just too simple to my adult mind. It was similar but not the same. I needed to challenge these new, more subtle fears as an adult in an adult world.

That's why the first time I saw Twain's powerful aphorism, I knew I had something I could use in my self-talk to remind myself at key times to go on, to go for it. So I immediately memorized the quote to energize me, to use as a spur, as a reset, when I was challenged by something to the point of fear. I started using it to encourage myself to do all sorts of things much more complicated than my old front flip.

This train of thought when cancer came into my life, using my self-talk, allowed me to own cancer rather than fear it. Maybe you have heard someone threaten another by clenching his teeth and saying, "I own you!" By "owning" my cancer, I developed a feeling I had control over it. This allowed me to act more calmly and with a feeling of strength in talking with myself, my family, friends, and even my doctors.

I pictured myself continually staring at my evil friend, my cancer, in the face. Keep your friends close—and your enemies closer. Each time, I knew I had to do the thing I feared the most: I had to fully engage my cancer again so it would die instead of me. I feared the operations, but I did not fear them for long. Time to take a run at this enemy with the help of a good doctor. Now.

As time has gone on, I've used this aphorism for things like public speaking and writing this book. While the fear was paralyzing at first, I grew to really like public speaking. And you have this book in your hand. Need I say more about the death of that fear?

Won't Back Down

I've tried to pass the skill of actively overcoming fear to my son, David Jr. He became quite a good soccer player in his high school years. In fact, he still plays every Wednesday night with a team in his neighborhood. One day during his junior high days, as we were driving to a local home game, I noticed he was unusually quiet. Gently, I asked if he had butterflies in his stomach. Surprised that Dad would know that, he said yes. Having dealt with and overcome those feelings many times as a school kid and more, I explained to him that his body knew he was going up against a challenge and it was getting him ready so he could be really sharp and play his best. I told him he should be glad he had butterflies.

I then turned on a Tom Petty song, "I Won't Back Down,"[1] from his *Full Moon Fever* album.

"I Won't Back Down"
Well I won't back down, no I won't back down
You could stand me up at the gates of hell
But I won't back down

Gonna stand my ground, won't be turned around
And I'll keep this world from draggin' me down
Gonna stand my ground and I won't back down

[*Chorus:*]
Hey baby, there ain't no easy way out
Hey I will stand my ground
And I won't back down

Well I know what's right, I got just one life
In a world that keeps on pushin' me around
But I'll stand my ground and I won't back down

Hey baby there ain't no easy way out
Hey I will stand my ground
And I won't back down
No, I won't back down

We sang it together, almost shouting it all the way up the hill to his soccer field. That day, it became a theme song for Dave and me. Over the years, when we have a challenge, whether together or apart, we may break out in song even to this day. There have been deaths of many fears over the years in our family.

This song has also been a personal anthem for me as I have faced down my cancer. I'm sure Tom Petty and Jeff Lynne, who helped him write it and sing it, would be happy to know that you, too, have adopted his song as your anthem. We've got just one life. Stand your ground! Thanks, Tom.

And yes, if you're wondering, now that I am over seventy, I have conquered not only my fear of cancer but also, once again, my fear of doing a flip. It ain't pretty, but I can still do it (sort of—it is edging back to the three-quarter flip I started with, so it is safest doing it into water!).

I am finding that later in life, being a conqueror becomes less about daring first-time physical challenges and more about growing older with grace. It is a reality that instead of challenging ourselves to try new things, it becomes our assignment to gracefully challenge ourselves to accept that which we can no longer do. Accepting the fearful costs attached to the gift of living a long life becomes paramount. We must face no longer being a great skier or basketball player—or gymnast. We must face illness and complicated life-extending operations with grace. One can still be competent even if hearing and eyesight are challenged.

Graceful Growth

As a young financial advisor in the first two years of my career, I needed every client I could attract. And in line with my belief that the common denominator of success was the deceptively simple "successful people do the things failures don't like to do," I did everything and more than any client asked of me. One of those things was to go to people's homes if they asked me, rather than demand that they come to my office, as some other advisors did. Because of this focus on "over-servicing," I started getting friendly referrals.

A lovely lady named Mrs. Helene Arnhym was the widow of a retired marine colonel in San Diego. She felt I had been a great help to her, so she referred me to a lady friend of hers who was recently widowed as well.

She was the wife of a navy retired admiral who had recently died. I had been an admiral's aide during part of my short four-year navy career, so Mrs. Arnhym figured I'd be immediately simpatico with Mrs. Florence Hartman. She was right. We had a great relationship for many years, and even though I became too busy to go over to Mrs. Hartman's home, I still did because she was such fun (she had been in the Ziegfeld Follies) and a model of a strong-minded lady, even though she missed her admiral.

She called one day to tell me she had been in a moderately serious car crash and asked that we postpone our meeting for three weeks. When the time came, she met me at her door and limped noticeably as we walked into the living room to begin our meeting. I asked her how her recovery was going and she launched into a soliloquy about her leg, her hip, her elbow, and more.

After a minute or two, she suddenly caught herself, stopped in the middle of a sentence, and, reaching for papers, said, "But you didn't come over here to hear an organ recital, did you?" I was so surprised by her statement, I laughed really hard with her then, and I still laugh now as I think of her wry, knowing smile as she spoke those words. She was a great lady, and she had just as great a sense of humor, too. That attitude kept her young for many more years. She conquered those years with fearless grace.

We must also face the terrible loss of our good friends. I watched my stepmother live to ninety-nine and a half. Wonderful as that sounds, her pain and sadness after losing two husbands, most all her best friends, one of her daughters, and my brother was a huge and fearful cost of her longevity. May I honor her by remarking how gracefully she absorbed and recovered from each and every one of life's blows.

As you know from another chapter, I value common sense and good judgment. So I imagine (sigh) those two traits will soon overrule my aggressive physical nature and, as I said above, the flip will be no more. Not because I have physical or psychological fear. Nope. I will have to overcome the fear of not being able to do things anymore. I must accept, with grace, that I no longer have the body I once had. I must overcome the fear of and perceived risk of inventing my new older self and still being worthwhile. I must not fear change but accept and embrace it.

There you go. Guess I am already self-talking and gathering strength to gracefully conquer the many challenges involved in the goodness of getting older. And no organ recitals from me, friends, I promise.

CHAPTER 18

OLIVIA'S CHAPTER

Her View of the 2010 Events after Retirement

Behind every great man is no one. The woman is three steps ahead.

—Bill Cosby

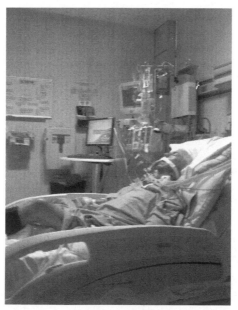

ICU for six days

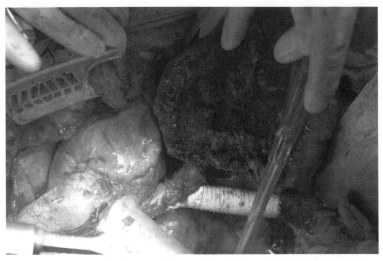

Dave's heart and new Gore-Tex vena cava

Note to you, dear reader. I asked the woman-three-steps-ahead to give her perspective on our recent eventful years.

Our story had a good ending, and we know that others do not. You've been reading Dave's version with his perspective. But typical of Dave, he wanted you to hear the perspective of another: a caregiver and spouse. He asked me to let you know what it is like to live with a person who is dear in your life who is mortally threatened with a potentially life-ending cancer. I can tell you only my story, and here it is, focusing on the events since his retirement.

The latest cancer chapter of our story began on Dave's sixty-fifth birthday in December 2009, when he retired after more than forty years in the workforce.

Dave had had intermittent and often excruciating pain in his right shoulder for several years. In 2000, he had a shoulder impingement surgery, so our initial thought was that the pain was something related to that. Over several years from about 2007 on, we tried to find an answer. We went to the shoulder doctor, who said it was not a shoulder issue and referred us to a neck doctor. The neck doctor said it was not a neck issue and referred us to a neurologist. He did tests and said it was not neurological, but he referred us to a neurosurgeon. That wasn't the answer, and he sent us back to the shoulder doc. This was interspersed with nerve-block treatments and days off work—and life—when the pain was excruciating. There was no reason for the pain and no answer.

At each appointment, we asked if it might be referred pain from a cancer, and the answer was always no. Referred pain is when you feel discomfort in an area that is not injured—and that confused everyone.

The saga continues to mid-December 2009, when Dave's primary care doctor sent him to a hematologist to investigate blood lab issues. That doctor did more blood work and told us she would be in communication after returning from a holiday vacation. We waited until the second week of January and finally called her—just to get an appointment later in January. Time was ticking by; pain, and now worry, persisted. We went to that appointment at a very chaotic and unattractive office, and the only response was to order an MRI. We waited to be contacted about a date and then had to push for that ourselves. Disappointed in the length of time and the chaos, we asked the primary doctor to refer us to another hematologist. When the MRI results were finally in, we visited that doctor, who began by telling Dave that the cancer was metastasized, only palliative care was possible, and that he had six months to two years to live. When we registered shock, he said, "Didn't anyone tell you that you have cancer again?" No! He was the first doctor we'd seen since the MRI. While anger was the emotion we could have chosen, we chose to focus on the problem and listen to the rest of his evaluation.

He said the only hope was some weird treatment involving radiological injections which would preclude any possibility of surgery later. So we talked to his referred radiologist about it in a messy borrowed office; it sounded too implausible and far-fetched for us to consider. As we walked out behind the doctor, he lit a cigarette. How offensive for a cancer (or any) doctor to do that.

Since he offered no hope, we decided to go back to M. D. Anderson in Texas, where the 1998 cancer was successfully treated. As we traveled there, we had hope again. It took several weeks to get all the medical records of the past ten years together and get an appointment.

But the response was similar: metastasized, not operable; maybe a course of chemo would help, though no studies had been done for more than ten years and then only of a tiny sample (in Italy), of which only one or two survived. There seemed to be no other choice—what a blow.

We went home and scheduled yet another trip to Texas in two weeks to start the poison. Poison it was, thirty-five pounds from Dave's 160 and total loss of hair and feeling sick a lot was no fun. The Texas hospital could not put in a port for direct injection of chemo, so he had a tube in his arm for injecting the monthly infusion, and that area on his arm became very red and infected with an open sore; he was allergic to the tape that held in the input tube. I had to clean the area daily and sterilize it. Day after day, lots of bandages and gloves and sterility.

It was cancer all day, every day—nothing but cancer. That was the new normal, and that was that.

I'm a pretty matter-of-fact person. Being overtly emotional would not have helped Dave or me. While I may be matter-of-fact, I lived most of my life with a lot of fear. But I had survived a divorce, abandonment, and years as a working single parent of a challenging child. I had shed so many tears during those heart-wrenching years that I had none left. If I could survive all that, I could certainly gather strength now to be there for Dave and survive this process. Much as Dave follows Alexander Pope's "all partial evil, universal good," I translate that as "shit happens, but overall, life is good."

I am comforted by information. Thank goodness for the Internet, as I read everything I could find about adrenal cortical carcinoma (ACC) and treatment options, of which there are few. The more I read, the more able I was to talk to doctors and help look for options.

Being busy also comforts me, so there were few idle hours. There was always work to do and exercise and reading. We both read a lot about cancer and diet and believed that we should do everything we could to take care of our bodies so that they would not be good hosts for cancer. I grew many of our vegetables and made yogurt and nutrition shakes. Diet and exercise and stress-reduction through time management and self-talk are keys to health—and what better time to try to be healthy than when you have cancer or are around someone who has cancer.

I walked two miles in our neighborhood with friends most mornings; getting out and getting fresh air and exercise helps a lot. I still do it to this day.

Dave and I share an acute sense of humor, so we both tried to find funny things in this new chaos, and occasionally, we did—and we found lots of frustrating things. We watched funny movies and tried to live a normal life. Dave continued to play golf with his friends as long as he could and even rode around the course with them a bit after that. (We live across the street from a small club course and have our own cart, so that made it easier.)

Dave got a wig, as he didn't want his newly bald head to be a reminder to his friends that he was sick. (This is another example of Dave's thinking of others rather than himself—he didn't want his friends to be uncomfortable.) When we stopped at a busy sandwich shop on one of our trips into town, we noticed that most of the young men had the shaved-head look, the new fashion, and he never wore the wig again.

There were lots of prayers, and I contacted friends around to world to ask for their prayers for peace and direction and healing. Those friends contacted their friends, and soon we had a large network across many countries. We believe in the power of prayer. Whether it was Confucian good thoughts or Judeo-Christian prayers or atheist/agnostic energy, we believed it would all come together for good. Even if Dave had not survived, those positive thoughts of so many people gave us both strength and energy. E-mails and cards arrived from people we'd never met bringing hope and love.

Dave began to sleep a lot, a good way to deal with pain and sickness, often with a dog on his lap. I was still working, albeit not much and all by computer, so during his naps, I worked and read and cleaned and did laundry and gardened. Time passed by quickly. We had a few visitors and found ourselves cheering them up rather than them cheering us. That was fine. Most of them came to bid farewell, expecting the worst—though they never said so.

We buoyed each other. Dave is an especially spiritual man and lives it every day, though we do not go to church regularly, by reason of our remote location. We do read the "Daily Word" and are not afraid of being faithful and quietly living it. We talked about music that he loved and what it meant to him, thinking that those choices would be included in a remembrance. His kids came to visit, and he gathered the strength to be Dad and share his love for them.

A big blow was the death of our beloved thirteen-year-old spaniel, Charlie, who was blind in one eye and gimpy in both forelegs. He had gone to work with us daily for five years, so his loss was huge. We had decided not to get another dog until the cancer travel to doctors and hospitals was over—positive thinking that it would end. One day, when we were about to start lunch, Dave asked, "Where's Charlie?" Then he remembered and started to cry. So we found online a rescue dog that looked like Charlie and drove the fifty miles each way to pick him up. His sister, a little shabby, fearful, black-and-white spaniel, looked at us with soulful eyes, so we decided to adopt her, too.

Dewey and Duchess

It is a big mistake to replace a beloved older pet so quickly, especially with two abused adolescent dogs. The girl dog had a submissive wetting issue and peed whenever and wherever she felt frightened, which was all the time. She hid behind her brother and was afraid even of love. The boy dog was coprophagic and ate everything, including his own feces and things he dug up in the yard. They were quite out of control, didn't know how to play, and barked whenever new people arrived. It was exhausting—not what we'd hoped for. Dave's son was a big help in understanding all that, but he lived miles away in Los Angeles and was busy with grad school, so he could not visit often.

The hospital in Texas had suggested that instead of going there each month for chemo, we could have the infusions done closer to home. We contacted hematologist number two, but he never got back to us—thank goodness, as he was convicted of using illegal foreign drugs on patients. We then contacted the UCSD Moores Cancer Center, which is only sixty-five miles away, as several friends had been successfully treated there and had great respect for it. The center was most accommodating. We went to see Dr. Fred Millard, who agreed to administer the infusions, and his wonderful nurse/case manager, Marianne Bowe, was able to get that port installed within two days. That was a huge relief to the pain and redness from severe inflammation in Dave's arm.

We spent three days each month in the outpatient chemo clinic. It was comfortable and bright. I talked to some other patients and their spouses and learned that everyone's journey is different. I talked several times to a lovely couple; the husband was being treated for lung cancer, though he'd never smoked. He had always done the right thing: diet, exercise, had a good military career, was an honorable man and good father. He seemed to be more accepting of the cancer than his wife, who was angry about it. It was harder for her than for me and, unfortunately, her wonderful, strong husband did pass away not too long thereafter. I think of her today and hope that she has found peace.

I developed a renewed interest in art history, so I read lots of books, researched wonderful online resources, and watched films online. I enjoyed that indulgence while Dave was in clinics and hospitals.

I reread Dr. Elisabeth Kubler-Ross's books on death and dying and the stages: denial, anger, bargaining, depression, and acceptance. (My mother had died of cancer and chemo in 1987; I'd read them then.) I felt so bad for that wife with her anger, but I certainly understood. Neither Dave nor I went through those stages, perhaps because we had lived with the cancer for so long and knew that every day had been an extra day, so we were grateful for that time.

Dave also *knew* that *if* we could find the right surgeon, everything would be okay. We are both big fans of Winston Churchill, the brilliant statesman who led the English in their darkest hour of Nazi bombings in World War II, saying, "Never, never, never give up!" and, "If you're going through hell, keep going." We lived by those words for months. And we never gave up.

At the end of May and the second month of chemo, we went back to Texas for an evaluation. What a horrible experience. We had a travel day, then a day of tests, then a waiting day, then, finally, the doctor appointment—but the doctor never showed up, though we waited three hours. The snippy assistant read from the computer screen but did not wait for any questions. We found out from an assistant that the doctor had left town while we were waiting and now would not take our call. We e-mailed our questions, but the reply was to ask for the name of the UCSD oncologist we were using and that she would send the answers only there. Rude, impersonal, and infuriating.

When we got back to San Diego, we asked Dr. Millard at UCSD to transfer all Dave's care there, and he agreed. Yeah! Whenever we had questions, a quick e-mail to Marianne and we had the answer. She is an angel on earth.

The next two months dragged by. Dave was weak and sick, and it was increasingly hard to be buoyant. Chemo brain had robbed him of some decision-making skill, and he saw me at times as Nurse Ratched, a role I had to take on. I was in control of food and medicine and took it seriously. No junk food, no Coke, pills on time. He finally, smartly, said, "I will do whatever you say," which I remind him of yet today.

I did all the chores and cleaning and putting out the trash. It actually made things easier, as I had no expectations of help. I did a little "bargaining," such as, "God, if you keep him alive, I'll never complain about this and that again." That is sometimes a hard one to keep now that he is alive and well.

Of course, I thought about what life might be without him. We'd been married only about thirteen years, though we had worked together and shared an office longer than that, so we knew each other quite well. We were financial advisors and had helped a lot of clients, many of whom were widows, to deal with estate settling, so that process was not a worry for me. I had been the one to pay the bills, so that was not a challenge either.

While those things worry many spouses in my situation, I was fortunate they did not worry me.

We live in a small neighborhood pretty far out in the country. The nearest grocery is thirteen miles away and nearest stoplight is thirty-five miles away. It is safe and serene, and our neighbors are caring and very social. When we moved out here, there were four widows who were good friends and were invited to every party, not the experience of singles of many city neighborhoods. Social life here is very inclusive. I knew I would be okay.

I also knew that Dave was very concerned about me and his two adult kids and didn't want to miss their growing and having kids of their own. But his greatest concern was not what he would miss but how their lives would be without him and if he had provided enough for them. He always thinks of the other person, not of himself. That is one of the many reasons why he is a good dad. He actually called each of them and was able to talk with them prior to the surgery he eventually had to assure them and share with them about the insurance he had for them and his love for them.

Distraction was a good thing, and during the weeks between infusions, when he was feeling good, we took a short trip. New scenery helped buoy his spirit.

At the end of the fourth month, the doctors ran the appropriate tests and discovered that nothing had changed—things were no better, but no worse. After Dr. Millard delivered that information, he followed it immediately by telling us that he had talked to Dr. Lowy, an oncology surgeon who was eager to meet with us. Less than a week later, that meeting happened. Dr. Lowy and his nurse/case manager, Debbie Soldano, were great. Of course, we don't remember all the details except Dr. Lowy saying that the risk of problems during surgery was about 30 percent—and, of course, we knew that without the surgery, the risk of death was 100 percent. We looked at each other. Not a big decision there.

Dr. Lowy wanted Dave to meet his colleague, a liver surgeon specialist who had been in San Diego less than a year. That meeting took place two days later. Dr. Alan Hemming walked into the exam room saying, "You know, you are really weird." Dave replied, retaining his sense of humor, "I've always thought of myself as unusual," to which Hemming replied, "Yes, but your case is really weird." We all laughed. Virtually no one lives with adrenal cortical carcinoma as long as Dave. (Only about 20 percent survive five years, and here it was, twenty-four years later.) Dr. Hemming drew on paper some of the things that might be done and quantified the risk of problems at 15 percent, confident but certainly not arrogant. We went home cheering with renewed hope.

The next month flew by, including meeting a cardiac surgeon, as the team of doctors thought they might have to cut the breastbone to reach the cancer in the diaphragm. On September 22, 2010, a team of six surgeons and many nurses and support specialists successfully removed all the cancer. They did cut the breastbone and closed Dave up with seventy-five staples from his throat to belly button and then right across to his hip. The lab reports came in a few days later that there were clear margins everywhere—so he was cancer-free.

A number of friends offered to sit with me while he was in surgery, and I dearly appreciated those offers. But I am the kind of person who would have felt that I had to be present and involved with them, so it seemed more a burden than support. That may seem a hard concept for some spouse/caregivers to understand, but that is the way I felt. During the surgery, I busied myself with seven or eight computer-based continuing education exams for my business that I had put off, so that time was uninterrupted and a good distraction for me. Just as I finished the last one, Drs. Lowy and Hemming came out to tell me the good news of a successful surgery and strong patient.

Dave spent the next six days in ICU on a lot of morphine, which caused nightmares of being kidnapped. There was a lot going on in his ICU room, lots of trees of saline and other drips, lots of beeping from computer monitors and the breathing apparatus. Because of the nightmares, he was restrained for several days until the morphine levels could be lowered and he was returned to consciousness. I spent every day by his side, fourteen to sixteen hours, just feeling that he needed an advocate on hand and also to see any doctors who came by on their odd-hour rounds. I read, studied, took long, brisk walks around the parking lots, watched movies online, and wrote e-mails of his progress.

I was staying with friends nearby who almost never saw me. We had a funny story when he was partially conscious and able to talk: he was still convinced that he had been kidnapped and was being held in a boat in San

Diego Bay (from the sound and color of the bubbling monitors and drips), so he called me close and said, "Here's the deal: we're going to make a break for it." I laughed out loud and asked him if he wanted me to push his bed to the elevator. He finally understood that he was in a hospital and not on a boat, and that calmed him. Curiously, he later told me that he had had the same dreams coming out of his 1998 cancer surgery with kidney removal.

Next came six more days of regular hospital care, starting to walk again and get the bodily functions going—that time flew by— and he was cancer-free! With his determination to live life to the fullest again, his recovery was strong.

Six months to the day after that miraculous surgery, we were skiing. I took a video of him skiing down through some light moguls, and we sent it to the doctors and nurses who had done such a great job and cared so much for us.

What advice can I give to another spouse caregiver?

1. If you do not know about your finances, begin learning *now*! I know from some of our clients that that can be the scariest part of life if things do not go as well as they did for Dave and me.
2. Watch your own diet and exercise, and be a role model and partner.
3. Find a new intellectual interest and take classes, watch movies, and read books on your computer.
4. Be an informed patient advocate.
5. Reach out to people who can be supportive; find resources at cancer centers.
6. Keep busy; the Internet is your friend. Take classes online through iTunes U, watch Netflix, expand a different part of your life.
7. Work with doctors and nurses you trust and who respect both of you.
8. Don't fall apart emotionally in front of your patient. Nothing good can come from it.
9. Respect your patient's wishes, but be realistic about chemo brain.
10. Remember that a lot of people survive cancer, but no one lives forever.
11. Be bold. Talk about the important things before it is too late; it might not be easy, but do it. Talk about your favorite music and

memories and photos and wishes, even for things like a memorial service. Write your own obituary and see if you are happy with your life.

12. Encourage your kids and others to maximize their schooling and work life to do the best they can so they can buy good insurance and have a comfortable financial cushion for these circumstances. Don't be afraid to remind them it's their responsibility, not that of the government.

13. If you "bargain" with God or whomever during the process, remember that afterward and keep your part of the bargain. ("God, if you will save him, I'll never be grouchy again about doing the dishes.")

14. Stay away from toxic people, even if they are family. Choose carefully with whom you spend time, without feeling guilty about it.

15. Keep calm and carry on.

16. Never, never, never give up.

This is actually not the end of the story. The incision from the surgery never healed properly, as there was surgical mesh from the 1998 surgery that poked its way through the abdominal incision. So in July 2011, he was opened up again, lots of infection and mesh were taken out, and the little bit of abdominal muscle that remained was reattached. That muscle repair did not last; he has no abdominal muscles on the right side, so no sit-ups, but fortunately, no negative effect on his golf game.

Then, while we were hiking in Utah in May 2012, Dave developed a subdural hematoma. He had a headache and wanted to stay in the car while I visited one last viewpoint. When I got back to the car about fifteen minutes later, he was in excruciating pain. I'd had a friend who had had a brain aneurysm, so I knew that a sudden-onset, excruciating headache was very serious. There was no cell signal where we were, about ten miles into Arches National Park, so I started driving and calling, hands-free.

When I got through to 911, I was told that I could get to the hospital faster than they could get an ambulance to me; I was there in about ten minutes.

I keep a list of Dave's med history on a page in my wallet, so when I gave that to the admit nurse and described the symptoms, they had him in a CT scan within ten minutes. They suspected the hematoma, but with no neurosurgeon on staff, they ordered a helicopter to fly him to Grand Junction, Colorado. We had to wait about an hour for the copter, and it was awful to watch him in such pain. The small chopper had room for just the pilot, two wonderful nurses, and the patient.

I watched them fly out and then packed up at our hotel and drove the two hours to Grand Junction. The speed limit is 75, a big relief in a case like that. When I got to the hospital, Dave was awake, alert, and hungry, as most of the pain had diminished. They kept him there on watch for three days, and then we drove home. (I need to interject that I am a very bad passenger, so I do most of the driving.) When we got home, we started another round with neurologists. He was told to be very still, no walking except around the house, no picking up anything heavier than a carton of milk. I was not a good enforcer, and he stretched the limits.

After about two weeks, his speech started getting fuzzier, and he began to forget names and words, and I thought perhaps it was early dementia. Unfortunately, that extra activity he had been doing caused another burst of bleeding, and he had to have two burr holes drilled in his skull to relieve pressure. He was alert enough to remember that his son was getting married in a few weeks and to ask that the doctors not shave part of his head so that he would still look normal for the wedding photos. The docs complied, shaved less than a square inch, and taped the hair aside, which was uncomfortable when the tape was removed, but his full head of gorgeous silver hair was intact for the photos. This time, he complied with activity restraints and was soon well again.

I continue to worry about what will come next. He is very good about staying in touch. He now also carries a copy of his medical history, and his friends know to contact me immediately if anything happens. We enjoy each day and feel very blessed to have this extra time. Every day for us is an extra day. Life is good!

CHAPTER 19

THE FINALE—EXCEPT IT'S NOT

(On stage) Sixty-eight-year-old Carolyn takes off her
towel and steps into the bathtub completely naked. The
cantankerous woman is dying of cancer and wants to die
sooner rather than later.
—From NPR review of the play *Dead and Breathing*,
July 19, 2014

You, dear reader, have spent a few hours looking fairly deeply into some
of the people and events that have shaped my life and how I responded to
and interacted with them, with particular focus on my four major cancer
challenges. You've even heard from my wife about what a character I am
(and she is). Thank you, Olivia, for the chapter—and for everything else.

So where does this journey leave us? Let's take a look.

A couple of months ago, a good friend who also was in the Vietnam
War said to me, "Dave, it's like you have four purple hearts from your
battles with cancer and you're still here to talk about it." The wise-guy part
of my self-talk wanted me to say, "You forgot about the subdural hematoma
and the stroke." Thankfully, my lips didn't move with that remark. Instead,
I truthfully said out loud, "Thanks. I never thought of it that way before."

A bit later, my friend's compliment bounced back up in my
consciousness. I thought about how I would have continued by explaining
why I think I'm still here. I think it might have come out of my mouth
(without the wise-guy factor) something like this:

As Eleanor Roosevelt said, "You gain strength, courage and confidence by every experience in which you really stop and look fear in the face. You are able to say to yourself, 'I lived through this horror. I can take the next thing that comes along.'"

My experiences early in my life, which were so horrific at the time, were actually endowing me with tools and methods of thinking that prepared me for the events that occurred later in my life. All of my seeming misfortunes have become opportunities for growth and understanding. I choose to see them that way.

Also, I have my faith wherein Pope's remarkable essay tells me "all partial evil" will eventually turn to the over-arching "universal good" in life when I exhibit true patience. I believe the My Chi approach accepts cancer into my life, and the accompanying self-talk creates in my mind a feeling of strength, which allows me to act with determination and peace of mind—a.k.a. courage—in the face of fear and in spite of the challenges involved. These are outlooks that sustained me through the near impossible and unavoidable low times and still do to this day.

I have kept these thoughts alive through my conscious management of my self-talk. And when I go off track— which I still frequently do, like any of us—my reset approach using trigger words, like a bright sign reflecting my headlights on a dark night, quickly directs me back to the main highway. There, I can reconnect with my primary goal of dying with this cancer, not from it and aspiring to a life with grace. To use one of today's popular sayings, which you now know I have adopted and use frequently, these approaches helped me "keep on keepin' on."

The doubt, fear, and sadness that arise from being told you have cancer or any other life-threatening disease are so powerful that you can become disoriented. As I said earlier, it is like a meteor hitting you. Life inexorably changes, in some ways forever. We humans in the twenty-first century are used to fixing things that are broken, and we want answers and solutions right away. On top of the doubt, fear, and sadness, we become frustrated and impatient with people and the process of trying to get well. But impatience is dangerous to our faith. We also tend to perceive most challenges, including serious illness, as a competition like *Monday Night Football*. And we're gonna beat the living (you know what) out of the challenger. We're going to win! We react.

But I believe the best thing we can do, like a lot of good things in this life, is counterintuitive. Use My Chi. Rather than conjuring up fighting, which creates even more fear and anger as by-products, as you know now, I choose to mentally model the form and actions of a physical t'ai chi master. For me, it's My Chi.

Adapt and Accept

I chose to adapt and accept that I had cancer coming right at me and that it was trying to kill me. Instead of throwing up defenses, I chose to invite my cancer into my space by "surrendering" to a stronger position. By my self-talk, I allowed myself to own my cancer. By owning it, I developed a feeling I had control over it. This, then, allowed me to act more calmly and with a feeling of strength in talking with myself, my family, friends, and even my doctors.

As you know, my reaction to my cancers has been to take Mark Twain's advice: "Do that thing you fear and the death of that fear is certain."

Once again, Twain encourages us to do something counterintuitive. The person heading for the morning shower may fear his meeting later in the day. Twain exhorts him to listen to himself and "Catch the fear!" Confront it and do something about it. He then can plan during his day to study his notes for the meeting a couple more times. That way, he redirects the energy from that fear to plan and do something that will make him successful, thereby reducing his fear. Knowing he will do this, he's able to calm himself in the shower. During his morning, he is calm, because he continues refocusing his fear-driven energy on solutions, not the problem. The mental discipline of resetting our self-talk when it goes negative gives us this huge lift.

These thoughts tie into my Professor Peter Drucker quote: "The best way to predict the future is to create it."

Action, when there is a problem—I prefer the word *challenge*—brings calmness. As I said, we humans like to fix things when they break. You've heard people say, "Don't just stand there. Do something!" And when we do something, we immediately feel better. This action is best directed when we establish meaningful goals. It's remarkable how long it takes us to complete something we're not working on. When we focus on a goal, good things happen.

I can remember times during my cancers when I would look over at Olivia and one of us would plaintively say, "I wish we could do something!" We were talking about my sickness, but soon we would realize there were plenty of small goals we could set. There were calls we could make. Or we could create an outing that would be wonderfully distracting for both of us. Exercise would make both of us feel better—except during my chemo. Whew.

There is almost always something to do, which is better than feeling fearful and sorry for ourselves.

I found looking outward rather than inward was a valuable way to drive my self-talk to "create my future" through action. My dad once said, "Son, be interested rather than interesting." I found that to be an especially useful thought to recall when cancer was so powerfully forcing me to look inward.

Take Time to Forgive; Let Go

Another action that may seem counterintuitive is the act of forgiving. It's counterintuitive until you realize the only one you are hurting by holding a grudge is yourself. Let go or be dragged. It is still a difficult thing to do even after coming to that understanding. Our self-talk tries to convince us anger and resentment are a good path because they have powerful immediate psychological rewards. Being "right" feels good. However, that reward creates pleasure, not longer-term happiness. What seemed positive turns negative. The pleasure is fool's gold. We feel righteous. We feel justifiably angry for being wronged, and it feels strangely good to be in the right. But would you rather be right for the moment or at peace and happy for your lifetime?

Negative feelings about others are anything but calming. They are not good for us. Our blood pressure can run up when we think about the way we were treated. We even lose sleep feeling "right" about being wronged. So the real loser is not the person at whom you are angry. The loser is you.

But with management of your self-talk, even if you don't believe yourself at first, you can start forgiving people, including yourself.

Like the word *water* on the golf course, your mind hears and focuses on what you're saying without judgment, e.g., "I forgive Bill for lying to me." For me, this eventually began to work with enough repetition. I started to do this active forgiveness thinking as an imperative. I first did this during one of those times when I knew there was a good chance I was going to die soon. I did not want to die carrying that anger with me. You can do this, too, but without the threat of dying to motivate you. Make that list and give it a try. Good luck to you. You may find it a noble effort for your benefit.

Grab Your Partner

Partnering is such a valuable concept to try to build into your life. Even if you think you are a loner, realize we are mammals and we tend to thrive on social experiences. Having people around us can make us feel better and live longer. As a simple example, it's a fact that married people live longer on average than single people.

Don't expect one partner to do it all or to be perfect for you. You may need several partners for different parts of your life: exercise partners, walking partners, diet partners, doctor partners, nurse partners, spiritual partners—your list may be long, and the partners will change, but they will all enrich your life.

My first wife Lori and I partnered effectively before marriage back in 1970. We had been dating for months and were serious to the point of planning to marry at some point, even though we were not engaged yet and didn't marry until 1974. We were having a great, great time with my fellow navy officers spending weekends going out to Long Island to visit Jones Beach during the summer, going skiing during the winter, and going on dates in New York City frequently. But we were smoking a lot, both of us. One Sunday, when I was visiting Lori and her dad at their apartment in midtown Manhattan, he spoke his mind and told us of the building research and evidence that smoking was really bad for our health. I almost don't believe it now as I look back, but we took his counsel to heart and made a pact that weekend. We both went cold turkey, quit completely, that day. I had been smoking for six years, but we were partners. We supported each other and we quit. Even though it was hard sometimes, we always had the other to remind us and provide support. It was startling to us, and wow, did her father think well of us. Partnering is powerful.

Psychoanalysts might find I was drawn to partnering to avoid the evil of loneliness after having lost my mom so early in life, and then my dad, and then my brother. They might say I was reacting and not wanting to ever again experience that loneliness and constantly being a bit scared. Okay, fine, but I have found such profound good from my partnering.

I find, over the decades using my five common denominators, that I have been a reliable judge as to who might or might not be a good partner for me when trying to meet a new or unfamiliar challenge. Whether in family life, business, quitting smoking, or just in the act of building true friendships through interactions like my golf group, partnerships have worked wonders for me.

In all those areas of my life, I feel I have accomplished so much more than I ever could have alone. My original marriage partnership, which started with wonderful times (and quitting smoking), helped us raise two wonderful children and created a strong foundation for our entire family. My constant partnering with my stepmother, Chief Gannon, Rich Zielony, Derryck Jones, and my book mentor/partner/friend, Don Wilcock, all added so much capability to what I contributed to our efforts. My business partnership and then marriage partnership with Olivia gave us a wonderful business experience and personal life.

When accomplishing something of value, it may seem we can go it alone, and if it's a business venture, we may want to keep all of it for the financial reward. As a brand-new financial advisor, I would have liked to have kept all of my new client Don's business. I'm sure even Don would have been happy to avoid the costs of partnering with financial advisors to increase his investing success, but he knew partnering with Rich and me would achieve much better results than he alone could have achieved. By partnering and sharing Don's business, I created a measurable benefit for Don, Rich, and myself.

Each of those people made my life so much richer. I learned from them and learned to count on them. They in turn learned they could count on me. That feels good and creates peace of mind. Having partners has always kept me going when challenges reared up that seemed insurmountable. It allowed me to be more adaptable. It was so valuable having a partner in those times to provide support and just to talk to, to provide perspective outside my own self-talk.

I have always viewed my efforts as not only for me but also for my partners. This feeling is not unlike the tease my father used to throw at me before sending me out to mow the lawn. He would say, "Now, if I told you to go mow your friend Jimmy's front lawn with him, you'd be excited." And grudgingly, as I went out the door, I would nod and say, "Yeah, Dad, I get it; you're right." There's something enriching to any experience when you are doing it with another. Golfers would love to have a hole in one at any time, but it is a much richer experience if you're with a foursome rather than when you are playing single. Each of my partners has added quality and richness to my life experience that still warms my heart as I think of them today. They are a huge part of the texture of my life.

Look Outward, Not Inward, for Healing

For those of us with cancer, we find the job of getting well so overwhelming it may cause us to turn inward, into our own minds, and spend quite a bit of time alone. And when we spend time alone when challenged by a death threat, it is astounding how our self-talk can conjure up all sorts of negativity. Some people pull away from friends in the process—just when they need them the most. This is not unlike a new widow going into seclusion to grieve rather than finding a way to be among her friends who could and want to lend support. You may remember this is exactly what my dad did after my mom died, much to our mutual loss. It was only after he reset and got the courage to reach out all the way to Ohio and ask his former college girlfriend to go out with him that everything in his and my life turned around.

There's an old Swedish proverb: "Joy shared is twice the joy. Sorrow shared is half the sorrow." Friends and partners can be magic. Reach out to people around you and be forthcoming about your disease and your experiences. Don't sit home alone and convince yourself that you are dying and no one wants to be around you. I know all the things we say in our self-talk: "I look terrible. I don't even want to get dressed to go outside today. I don't feel well enough to do what my friends asked." *Stop. Reset. Flip right-side up.*

Faith Enables Determination

Please. Use your faith and determination, and find a friend or partners to share your condition, your life. And don't wait for them to call. It never hurts to ask. Pick up that hundred-pound phone and make the call to initiate something: lunch, dinner, a movie. It will do wonders for you and them. Because of this discovery in my own situation, I'm still sitting here today lucky enough to tell you what I know to be true.

Docs as Partners

Imagine how grateful I am for the self-talk that drove me to use the concept of partnering with my doctors. I wanted to live, and they knew it. I did the things my doctors told me to, and they were pleased by my efforts. A professional firefighter in my neighborhood told me awhile back that as crews assess a neighborhood burning in a wildfire, they are often faced with the sad reality that they cannot save all the homes on the street. He said he and his fellow firefighters have to decide which houses to make primary efforts to save.

The way they do that is to look at the houses where owners have taken care to follow suggestions about fire resistance, because that increases the chance that firefighters can save the house. If they see a property that has plants and trees right up to the house and next door is a property where flammable vegetation has been cleared for a hundred feet around the home, they will fight to save the home of the owner who has created the clearance.

Doctors are interviewing us, just as we do them. They want to determine how likely we are to survive our illness—and how much we want to. In other words, they are looking not only at our physical condition. They are looking at our mental condition, our attitude, and our willingness to partner with them to succeed in an effort to save or prolong our life.

A willingness to partner with them clearly comes through and makes a difference in many doctors' minds.

Find Your Partner for a Task—Even Just One

One more thing about partnering for those of us who now have or have had cancer and fear its return. I have my dear wife and partner, Olivia, whom you now know has saved my life several times and is always there as a wonderful confidante. But we are not all so fortunate to have that partner built into our lifestyle. The next time you come upon a person struggling with cancer, look at them and ask yourself with your self-talk, "Would it benefit this patient if I offered myself to be a partner in some way?"

Your version of the partnership can take on the assignment that you and s/he devise. It doesn't have to be a constant care, life-saving situation. You may know or find out that the person is missing meals, and you can quietly offer to accompany him or her to a restaurant or bring in a lunch or dinner. Or it may be just having a conversation with that person once in a while. Remember the Mitch Albom book, *Tuesdays with Morrie?* When one partners, two benefit—and maybe many more.

It Never Hurts to Ask

My point here about partnering, whether regarding cancer or not, is that it never hurts to ask. I hope my suggestion to look for a cancer partner sticks in your mind, but there is a broader aspect of the concept "it never hurts to ask." When my son, David Jr., was about six or seven, he came into the kitchen where his mom and I were talking while she was fixing us dinner. Davey—that's what we called him at the time—had seen a toy that one of his friends on the street had come home with and was quite excited. "Dad and Mom, could I please have some money to buy one of those?" he asked as politely as he possibly could, knowing that he increased his odds by doing so. He had me with the "Please," softy that I am.

So I looked over at Lori and said, "Do you think it might be time for Davey to have an allowance?" Lori and I had a standing agreement regarding raising our kids that we would always support one another when they were present. When she saw the look on my face, she smiled a knowing smile as she replied, "Sure, great idea."

I have always used a money clip in a front pocket because I hate sitting on a wallet. I reached in and made a big deal of pulling out my money clip. I asked Davey what he thought the toy cost, and of course he didn't know, but I had an idea, and I wanted to give him less so he would have to save a couple of weeks to get it. I pulled out a five-dollar bill and handed it down to Davey, whose eyes at the time were just above the level of my belt buckle. He beamed and said, "Gee, thanks, Dad!" He then glanced at my money clip and back up at me as he said, "But could I have that one instead?"

To my utter surprise, he was pointing at the twenty-dollar bill I had on the outside of the other bills in my money clip. I was stunned for a moment, and then an idea flashed through my mind. I reached for the twenty, pulled it out, and handed it to him. As I took the five back, I looked him in the eye and said, "Sure, Davey. It never hurts to ask." Now he was the one stunned. He has never forgotten that lesson and still uses it as motivation to go on and "ask" today.

So don't let any negative self-talk tell you the person won't accept your offer or that you'll be embarrassed if s/he doesn't want you to become some version of a partner as they confront the many challenges surrounding an experience with cancer. Give it your best shot, but make sure you mean it before you offer. And if you do, what a wonderful gift to them—and you. When one partners, two benefit. Get involved.

Full Circle

In the beginning of this book, I told you one of my secrets: my five favorite "centering" aphorisms. My self-talk uses these to "flip my kayak back up" as quickly as possible when rough waters upset me.

1. Do the thing you fear the most and the death of fear is certain. —Mark Twain
2. Obstacles are those frightful things you see when you take your eyes off your goals. —Henry Ford
3. I will die with this cancer, not from it. —David Bantz

4. The best way to predict the future is to create it. —Professor Peter Drucker

5. Keep on keepin' on. Or as Winston Churchill said long before me, "Never, never give up!"

Do you see a commonality in my aphorisms? For me, they are a reminder that we are best off if, without surrendering our morals, we adapt to the unpredictable events occurring minute by minute, hour by hour, and day by day in our lives and focus on what they mean for our future. Conquer; don't complain about the past. This is My Chi, thinking on our feet, in the moment. It is at our great expense that we take much time to regret the past. All partial evil at the moment, universal good in the long run—if we are patient. We must live in the present and do what we can by our current actions to predict that there will be good in our future. Touch the white walls until you find an opening, and rejoice in your eventual discovery.

We sometimes allow ourselves to think we are in control of our lives. This is valid thinking for short periods of time, and I believe we must make the best choices during those times. As I have noted, UN Secretary Dag Hammarskjold said long ago, "We are not permitted to choose the frame of our destiny, but what we put into it is ours." E+R=O. Events *will* occur. Be your own best friend, and actively make decisions to try to make the outcome the best it can be.

Rather than end your day saying to your friends, "Guess what happened to me today?" I hope you begin saying, "Guess what I did today?" How we (R)espond is what determines the final (O)utcome, not the (E)vent itself. Dag Hammarskjold and Jack Canfield, however diverse their careers, had it figured out. May we learn from their observations that what we put into our lives is ours to choose.

Every one of us will die someday. Here's a final suggestion or two.

Live your life with vitality and commitment, whether you live a long life or cancer does become your harbinger of death.

Regardless, commit each morning to live your life as you wish; on purpose, with grace, and with thanks in your heart. We who have cancer have the "gift" of being made aware. We must cherish every one of the 86,400 seconds of each day and live our entire lives to the fullest.

Tomorrow morning, when you awaken and see the ceiling in your bedroom, before you do anything else, smile at your gift. You have another day! Then you can get up and go with true peace and thanks.

Don't sweat the small stuff—and after the gift of waking up, it's all small stuff, when you think about it.

As we all know, there will be that time when morning will never come. I leave you with a couple of final quotes to ponder. Let's start with one of my favorites, for who can say something about a well-lived life better than the creative genius Leonardo da Vinci.

As a well-spent day brings happy sleep, so a life well spent life brings happy death.

—Leonardo da Vinci

In 1932, Bishop Charles Henry Brent wrote the following beautiful eulogy known by some as *What is Dying?* using a ship sailing away as a metaphor for a person disappearing at death. As a former navy guy, I really relate and hope it is meaningful to you.

A ship sails and I stand watching till she fades on the horizon and someone at my side says, 'She is gone.'
Gone where? Gone from my sight, that is all. She is just as large now as when I last saw her. Her diminished size and total loss from my sight is in me, not in her.
And just at that moment, when someone at my side says she is gone, there are others who are watching her coming over their horizon and other voices take up a glad shout - There she comes!
That is what dying is. The horizon is just the limit of our sight. Lift us up, O Lord, that we may see further.

Here are the last few lines of a poem with similar perspective written by a remarkable legal scholar and writer, Rossiter Raymond, in 1928:

"Life is Eternal; and love is immortal; and death is only a horizon; and a horizon is nothing save the limit of our sight."

(Note: In 1990, it was built into the lyrics of a lovely popular song sung by Carly Simon. However, taking nothing from Bishop Brent, Mr. Raymond, or Ms. Simon, these exact lines actually originate from a prayer written more than two hundred years ago by William Penn, 1644-1718)

And for my final quote, of course I must remind you of part of "An Essay On Man," where Alexander Pope writes:

"Man knows so little. We are not the architects of our existence. We must wait to judge the meaning and the value of events in our lives."

Patience

Whether you are involved in a cancer situation or are dealing with some other struggle in your life, as we all are:

Above all, be patient with yourself and those around you, dear reader.
And expect answers eventually will come in the form of good.
They may not be what we expect,
But we will understand them in the fullness of time.
Never give up expecting the best.

AFTERWORD:
AND THEN THE PHONE RANG

On Monday morning, December 21st, 2015, Olivia and I were still in the bedroom with coffee talking about our day and the week ahead. They were to be filled with activities as this was Christmas week.

The phone rang and being closest, I picked it up. It was my oncologist, Dr. Millard. This was not surprising as I had just had my five year MRIs last week. Dr. Millard's "Hello Dave "was tired and ominous. He got right to it as he quietly said, "David, I just finished my review of your MRIs from last week. I'm afraid the news isn't good. We see a sizable, ten centimeter (four inches) mass on your remaining left adrenal gland. Your cancer had returned."

Deep breath. Act, don't react. That was my self talk before saying in my best My Chi form, "Okay Doctor, I am not surprised as I have always believed I will always live with this cancer until I die of something else. What shall we do?"

I put him on the speaker phone so my startled Olivia could hear the rest of the call. Of course, as a pro, he went right into the whole process ahead with PET Scans and seeing lead surgeon from 2010, Dr. Lowy as soon as possible to discuss the possibility of a surgical solution once again.

It is now December 24th, Christmas Eve and life goes on. Olivia and I have chosen not to tell our kids and friends yet. Why do that and potentially upset them before all the Christmas celebrations? I have my appointment with Dr. Lowy on the 29th and hopefully he will have the "good" news that he can operate.

If so, there goes my golf game again! Darn it!

I am not fearful and I don't think Olivia is either. We will accept and adapt to news and events as they unfold. This time, we are finding that fear is not one of the challenges we are encountering. What a gift.

179

ACKNOWLEDGMENTS

I am a fortunate man. By now, you know why I say that. But I must thank profusely the doctors who gave me remarkable advice and who performed the marvelous surgeries over the years that kept giving me back my wonderful life. In 1986, then Chief of Surgery for Scripps Hospital, Dr. Brent Eastman, with Dr. David Hall assisting, were instrumental in my survival of my first cancer challenge. Ten years later, Dr. Dana Launer did a marvelous job of keeping me around. He became a client and friend. Unfortunately, of all things, cancer took him from us a year or so ago, and all who knew him miss him.

In 1986, Dr. Jeff Lee of M. D. Anderson did a very difficult surgery, saving my life with his skill and intellect. When I received the news in 2010 that I was in for another challenge even greater than those before and after a major but fruitless search, it was Moores Cancer Center, UCSD, oncologist Dr. Fred Millard who saved the day. First, he was willing to help me out of a tough spot with my chemotherapy, and then he contacted Dr. Andrew Lowy, who put the fantastic team of doctors together to achieve what some at the center called a Christmas miracle. Drs. Alan Hemming, Andrew Lowy, Michael Madani, thank you for being there, and thank you for what you do and the marvelous work you performed on me. The skill and dedication you demonstrate every day you go to work dazzles me. May you be blessed, as I have been for knowing you.

Finally, where doctors are concerned, Dr. W. Wayne Hooper, excellent pulmonologist for many and most, but by my good fortune, my personal doctor and closing on thirty-year friend, thanks is not enough. I owe you my life. Then I owe you my life again. And then I owe you my life once again, Dr. Hooper, as you know by your reading, discovered the original cancer back in 1986, and we became friends. I remained his patient through recovery of that surgery, and our relationship quite simply has never ended. Wayne has acted as my personal physician since 1986, and he has found the resurgences of my cancer each time. Thank you, Doctor Hooper. I trust you with my life—for obvious reasons.

I am so fortunate to be married to a wonderful lady named Olivia, who plays a key role in my life journey as wife, lover, caregiver, partner, and best friend. At my request, she wrote her chapter that tells our story from her very different viewpoint. I cannot thank you enough, Olivia, for all of your gifts, including your invaluable assistance in creating this book.

I am also a fortunate man because I have been given the motivation to write this book by my high school friend, Don Wilcock, a seasoned, excellent writer for numerous publications over forty years. Don and I have talked for an hour or so almost every Friday morning for more than two years. During those calls, Don has mentored me beautifully. Sometimes he has led me, and sometimes he has driven me to an understanding of the art and skill of writing to enable me to express myself to you. He has been my Sherpa as I have climbed the mountain of writing my first book.

Finally, while I am fortunate for Don's and my wife's gifts of knowledge and time, we are all grateful for the opportunity to exercise our collective belief that we may give readers a way to live successfully even when a dreaded disease like cancer is woven into the fabric of their lives.

AUTHOR BIOGRAPHY

Four-time cancer survivor, David Bantz lost both parents before he was 17 and a big brother only in his 40s. Yet, in 70 years of life he achieved a Masters in Business, served his country for four years as a Navy officer and enjoyed a thriving 33-year career as an advisor and manager in the financial services industry. Now his wife and he are enjoying a happy retirement in the mountains of Southern California near San Diego.